Jesse Beery

A practical system of colt training:

also the best methods of subduing wild and vicious horses: With illustrations

showing modes of procedures and the requisite applicances

Jesse Beery

A practical system of colt training:
also the best methods of subduing wild and vicious horses: With illustrations showing modes of procedures and the requisite applicances

ISBN/EAN: 9783337713843

Printed in Europe, USA, Canada, Australia, Japan

Cover: Foto ©ninafisch / pixelio.de

More available books at **www.hansebooks.com**

—OF—

COLT TRAINING;

—ALSO THE—

BEST METHODS OF SUBDUING WILD AND VICIOUS HORSES.

BY JESSE BEERY.

WITH ILLUSTRATIONS,

SHOWING MODES OF PROCEDURE AND REQUISITE APPLIANCES.

Entered according to Act of Congress
in the year 1896,
BY JESSE BEERY, OF PLEASANT HILL, OHIO,
In the Office of the Librarian of
Congress,
At Washington, D. C.

PRESS OF
THE PARMENTER PRINTING CO.,
LIMA, OHIO.

TABLE OF CONTENTS.

	PAGE.
Introduction	6

CHAPTER I.
Colt Training.. 10

CHAPTER II.
Subjection... 29

CHAPTER III.
Kicking.. 45

CHAPTER IV.
Balking.. 65

CHAPTER V.
Shying... 75

CHAPTER VI.
Running Away.. 83

CHAPTER VII.
Bad to Shoe... 87

CHAPTER VIII.
Halter Pulling.. 101

CHAPTER IX.
Description of Appliances..................................... 107

CHAPTER X.
Promiscuous Vices... 116

CHAPTER XI.
The Overcheck and Curb Bit................................... 141

CHAPTER XII.
Teaching Tricks... 152

CHAPTER XIII.
Personal Experiences.. 171

CHAPTER XIV.
Testimony of Others... 187
Timely Facts and Maxims....................................... 236
Appendix.. 240

INTRODUCTION.

My object in publishing this book, is to teach persons who desire to learn, how properly to train a colt, and to give some practical points and ideas in subduing and educating horses that have acquired bad habits, viz: Kicking, Balking, Shying, Running away. Halter Pulling, and vices of every description, that horses are so liable to fall into when they are improperly handled.

The brutish man whose coarse nature makes him desire to beat, jerk, kick, swear at, and otherwise ill-treat his horse, will find nothing in this book to encourage him to continue his brutal treatment, and will therefore not find anything to interest or profit him. The only hope I have of that man is, that I may sell him a book (at the regular price) and that the book may fall into the hands of his sons, and that they may know more at sixteen than their father at forty; and thus save many a colt from abuse and being worthless.

The plan I use in teaching my System of Colt Training and demonstrating the different methods of subduing vicious horses is as follows: I have a large tent that I instruct classes in. I then take a green colt (one that has never had a bridle on) of some one of the scholars and give it its first few lessons before the class, to teach the class my system of training, and to show them how fast a colt will learn, and how well it will remember its training when given short lessons and taught but one idea at a time. In connection with teaching my system of colt training, I would demonstrate methods of subjection upon all kinds of vicious horses, and if there were any extremely ugly, bad horses in the country, those were the ones that were brought out for treatment.

These are only object lessons for you; to learn how to do it you must do it yourself. It is the purpose of this book by short and clear directions, and by the illustrations, to aid you in putting into practice what you learn and have seen or will see me do.

To profit by what you learn you must necessarily put your learning into practice. The man who can read and write, and does not read and write, is only equal to him who cannot read and write. If you learn how to educate a horse, you and the horse will not be benefited unless you educate him. But if you teach and educate him properly, he is the more willing, and at the same time more valuable servant, and you a happier and wealthier man. The horse is a servant, and his value depends upon his docility, willingness, ready obedience, beauty, speed, strength, and endurance, in about the order named.

The horse can be taught words of command only by associating them with an action, as we have only the whip and lines as the principal means for teaching the commands necessary for him to know. If he has confidence in his master, and understands what he wants of him, he will be ready and willing to obey every command that is given him. But if you say Whoa! when you want him to go slower, when you don't want him to scare and when he is standing perfectly quiet, how is he to tell what Whoa! means? Is it strange that you shout and yell "Whoa!" in vain when the horse is frightened and you in danger?

Nearly all men that keep tractable and well-trained horses, are good, kind hearted men, men who never lie to their horses or deceive them by giving commands in such a manner that they cannot be understood. I believe it will not be saying too much for my experience and observation, that in a number of instances I can tell the disposition of a horse by looking at the man that owns him.

With these few suggestions and observations I put forth this little manual, fondly hoping that it will benefit both horse and owner wherever it may be read.

INTRODUCTION.

I deem it not out of place here to mention the fact that all the appliances necessary in training colts and subduing vicious horses are manufactured and kept in stock by me, and can be obtained by writing to my address for particulars or ordered directly from the advertisements at the end of this book. My long experience in using and making these appliances is sufficient evidence that they are as nearly perfect in detail of construction as is possible. By buying them of me you will avoid the difficulty and inconvenience of trying to make them yourself or having your harness maker construct them from any description I might give in this book. For this reason the complete descriptions of these articles have been omitted.

Very Truly,
JESSE BEERY.

COLT TRAINING.

CHAPTER I.

Fear is the principal motive which causes the colt to resist training. It is natural for him to kick against an unknown object at his heels, to pull his head out of the halter as from a trap, and if of a bad disposition, to strike and bite if he does not thoroughly understand you. His fear is governed by his sense of touch, sight and hearing; and it is through these senses we obtain a mastery, and at the same time remove his fears of the halter, the robe, the harness and the wagon. These are the fixed laws which govern the actions of all horses, and the training of a colt is merely teaching him not to fear the working apparatus, but to fear and respect his master, and to obey his commands as soon as he has learned their meaning. Each one of these senses must be educated before the colt is trained. A colt's education may be compared with that of a child to a great extent. A horse is, of course, a dumb brute; and his reasoning powers are limited to his past experience. So we must reason with him by acts alone. Hence the importance of beginning every step with the colt right; for by our acts he learns. The successful school-master aims first to teach the child to have confidence in him. Hence the first lesson we give the colt is simply to teach it to have confidence in us and that we are its best friend and don't intend to hurt it.

FIRST LESSON.

Turn it loose in an enclosure about twenty-five feet in diameter, (I prefer a barn floor or a large carriage house, having vehicles and all obstacles removed,) take an ordinary buggy whip in your right hand, and go into the enclosure with the colt. Snap the whip a few times; the colt will run to get away from you; when it finds it is penned up and can not get away, it will then look to you for protection. Then approach him quietly; if he turns his heels to kick you or run away from you, give him a crack with the whip around the hind legs; follow this up until he will keep his head toward you; then throw the whip under the left arm and step forward and caress him on the shoulder; handing him a little oats, corn or apple, will assist greatly in winning his confidence. (However, I prefer to use nothing but caresses on the point of his shoulder.)

Let me also insist on the value of patience, from the very beginning of training a colt. Start out with the determination to keep cool yourself, whatever the colt may do.

It is to be expected that in his ignorance of what you want of him, he will try your patience, but what of that? You have all the advantage, and he is at your mercy.

Do not degrade your manhood by unjust violence toward an inoffensive subject, that is trying to understand and willing to obey you.

In following the above directions you will find that the wildest colt will follow you like a dog in twenty or thirty minutes; which I claim is the most important lesson given the colt.

SECOND LESSON.

Take it into the inclosure, put on it an open bridle with a straight bar bit, and no rein; next, put on a surcingle or the skeleton part of the harness, and run the lines through the shaft bearers of the harness.

This brings the lines below the hips, which will prevent the colt turning his head toward you; now you are in a position to teach the colt the use of the bit, and also the command, "Get up." The first five or ten minutes allow the colt to go about as it pleases; then begin to draw on the lines a little, and teach it to turn to the right and left. When you want the colt to start use nothing but the words, "Get up." "Horses can be taught words of command only by associating the command with an action." Hence when you say "Get up" to the green horse, you must give him a tap with the whip just as you give the command. He will

COLT TRAINING. 13

soon start when he hears "Get up" to avoid the stroke. Thus he learns the true meaning of the command. In this lesson you should teach nothing but the words

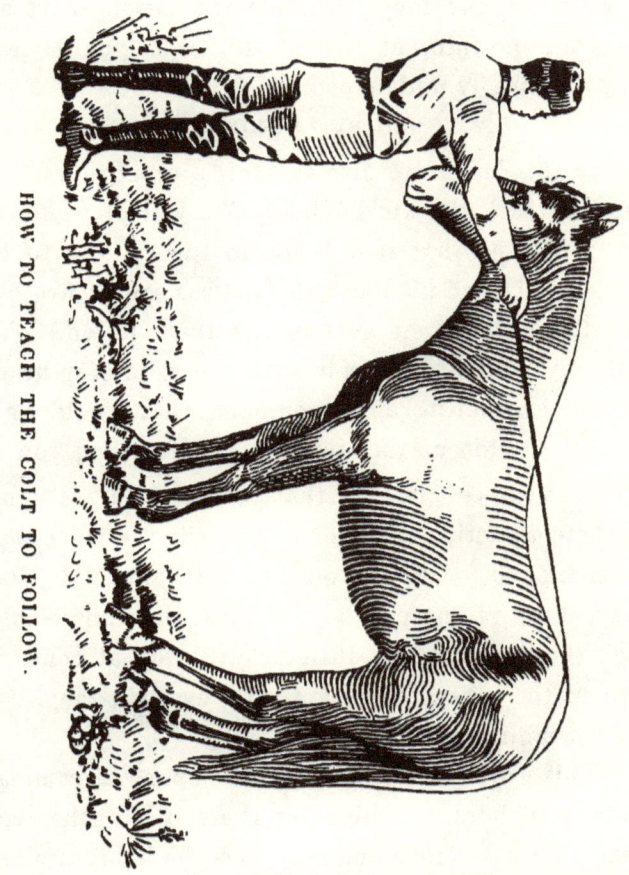

HOW TO TEACH THE COLT TO FOLLOW.

"Get up" and the use of the bit. The great mistake

that most men make in breaking their colts is, they try to teach them too many things at once. A colt will learn more in one hour per day, than it will in six hours or any longer. Make the lesson short and teach but one thing at a time. But what you do teach have thoroughly understood.

THIRD LESSON.

In this lesson we give the colt a repetition of bitting and teach the word Whoa! We will presume that the trainer has not said Whoa to the colt up to this time, (but I have no doubt that he has said it five hundred times before he gets to the third lesson.) You could say Whoa! to the colt until you were gray headed without associating an action, and that would never teach it to stop at the word. The first time you say Whoa! to the colt be sure that you are in a position to associate an action in order to teach it the meaning of the command. Just as you give the command Whoa! give a sharp raking pull on the lines; then immediately slack the lines; repeat until he will stop at command without the action; then you will have him taught the right meaning of Whoa.

This word Whoa, is the most important command we have in horsemanship; yet there is no other command that is so much abused. It is the habit of almost everybody, when handling colts or horses, to be continually using Whoa, Ho! Ho!, without any meaning whatever. If you want a horse to obey your commands, you will never lie to him or deceive him by giving commands when you don't intend to have him obey them. I dwell upon this command because of its importance. Quite frequently your lives may depend on a hearty Whoa! I can truly say that in my experience of handling colts and vicious horses, that my life would have been at stake hundreds of times, had it not been for having a well understood Whoa upon my horses. If you are careful in teaching this command, and practice firmness in two or three lessons, you will have a horse that will stop at the word Whoa under all circumstances and in any excitement.

FOURTH LESSON.

Give this lesson yet in the enclosure, as we have a number of advantages of the colt that we would not have outside.

First: If the colt wants to act stubborn and tries to get away from us, we can control it much quicker and easier than we otherwise could.

Second: There are not so many objects to take the colt's attention. A horse can think of but one thing at a time. The school-teacher can not teach his pupils anything while they are looking out the window, neither can you teach the colt anything while

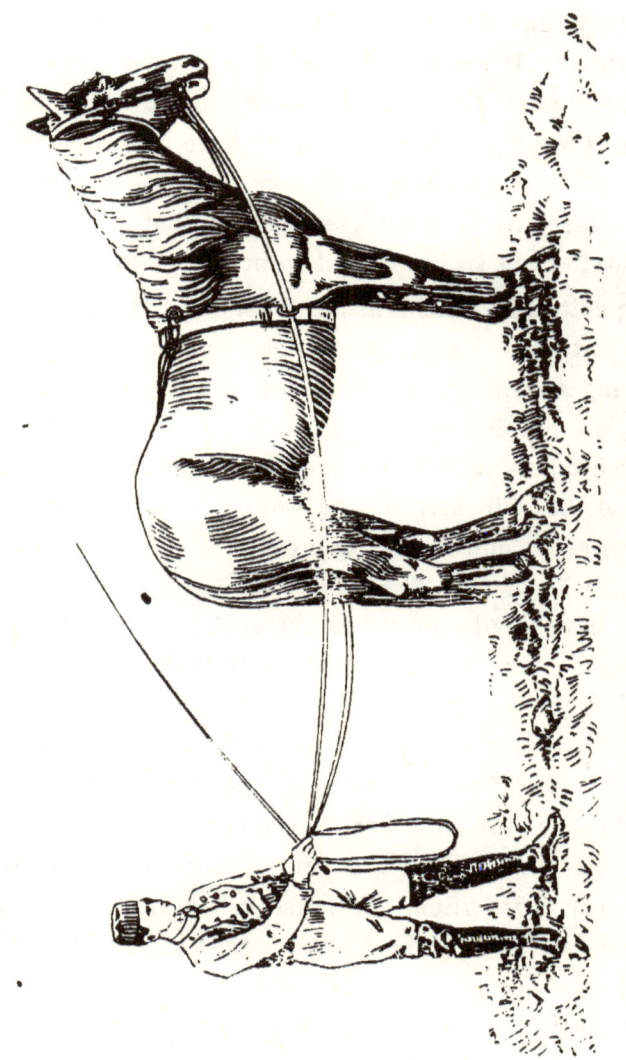

TEACHING THE COLT THE USE OF THE BIT.

he is trying to get to other stock, or having his attention attracted by chickens or a bit of paper flying up about him. While you have the colt in the building or inclosed lot you are not annoyed with the many things that are liable to take the colt's attention out-

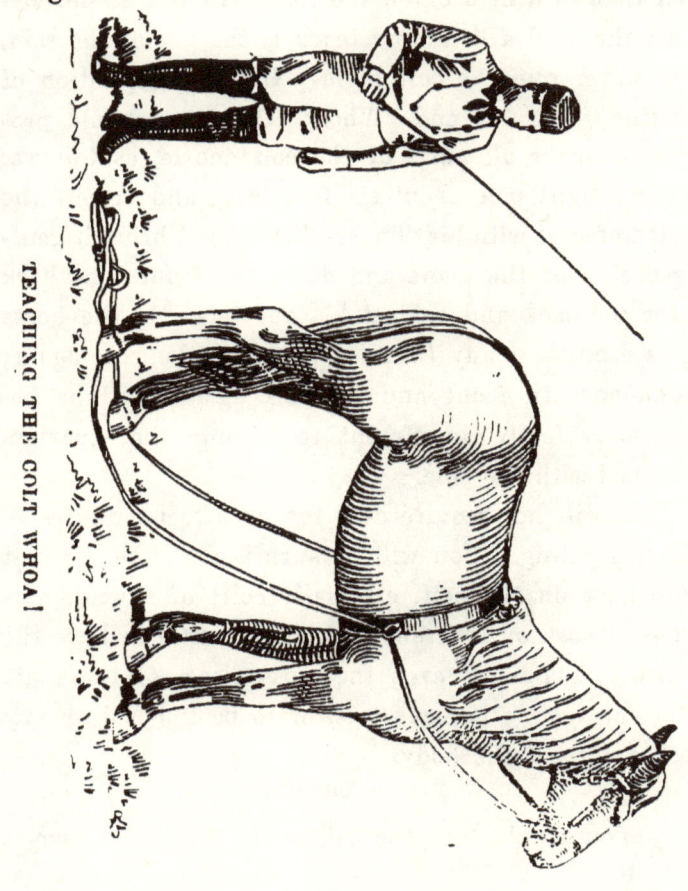

TEACHING THE COLT WHOA!

side. Persons who have not tried training colts in a building or limited inclosure will be agreeably surprised to see how much more control they will have and how much easier colts can be broken in this manner than in a field or on the road. In this lesson elevate the head a little and teach it the use of the rein, but never rein the colt high. Give it a repetition of bitting, "Get up" and "Whoa;" then you should proceed to make all parts of the colt gentle, as follows: Take a light pole about six feet long, and permit the colt to feel it with his "fingers," (his nose) bring it gently back over the mane and down the front legs, back over the back and against his quarters. If the horse gets excited at any time let him feel the pole again; commence in front and go back again until he becomes perfectly indifferent to having the quarters touched with the pole.

It will not require over ten or fifteen minutes to do this poling. You will be surprised at the effect it will have on the colt, especially colts of a wild, nervous disposition; thereby making it gentle to have the harness, chains, or even the cross pieces of the shaft to come against the quarters, or to be touched on any other part of the body.

FIFTH LESSON.

You should take the colt on the road and give it

a repetition of the previous lessons; at first it will act as though it had not been taught any thing, but a little firmness will make it as gentle and obedient outside as it was in the enclosure. Now you have a good foundation laid for driving. Next familiarize the colt with the vehicle, by having an assistant pull the vehicle around a few times behind the colt, and allow it to feel of it, and examine it according to his own way of reasoning. I would advise hitching the colt single first, and he will be no trouble to drive double.

POLING THE COLT.

However, you may use your own pleasure about that; but under all circumstances give the above lessons first. If you wanted to teach a dog to drive cattle, you wouldn't get an old dog that would run in front of the cows and chase them wherever you didn't want them; nine chances out of ten, the young dog would be like the old one. It would be natural for him to learn more from the old dog than from your teaching. For that reason I prefer to educate the colt by itself. It is very common for a man to hitch his colt first, without any training at all, by the side of an old farm horse that is lazy, possibly blind in one eye, and so old that he is listless. When you have this nervous, excitable colt harnessed by the side of the old slow horse, you then take your lines and ask your team to go. The colt plunges ahead; the old horse having spent many days in the harness takes life very easy and gradually gets in motion. The colt comes back and the load don't move. The next time you ask them to go the old horse moves ahead, the colt sets himself back in the breeching. Now you are in a good position to teach your colt to balk. If you will take the colt away from the old horse, and teach him by our system of training to drive single first, you will have no trouble to drive him double. The first time you hitch the colt up, if it is wild or inclined to be doubtful, it is advisable to use a single foot strap;

COLT TRAINING.

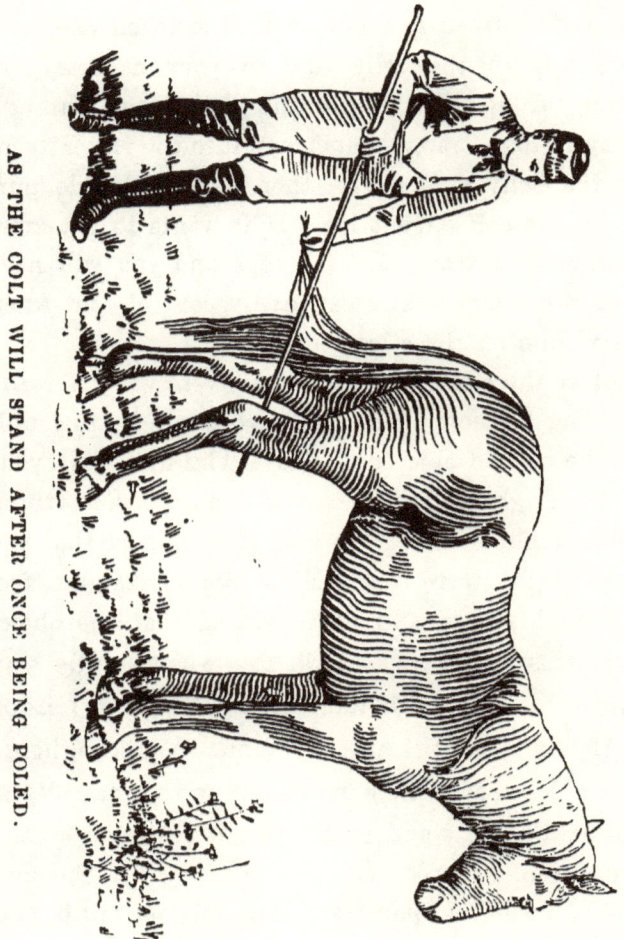

AS THE COLT WILL STAND AFTER ONCE BEING POLED.

buckle a foot strap with a ring in it, round the off front foot below the fetlock joint; next take a half inch cotton rope, fifteen feet long with a snap on one end; have a ring in the belly-band of your harness, run the snap through the ring at the girth, down through the ring in foot strap, up, and snap into the ring attached to the belly-band. You then have a double purchase on the colt's front leg. If it wants to get away or turn around, draw on your rope and you will have him on three legs. You can easily control him when you have him on three legs.

After these lessons have been given, you are ready for driving the colt. Your next work will be to familiarize the colt to objects of fear. The first time your colt gets frightened at a stone, stump, or anything else that might be along the road side, be sure that you take him right up to it and allow him to examine, feel of it with his nose, and be convinced that the object is harmless. In order to do this successfully you should talk to the colt like this: "Take care! Look out! Be easy, It will not hurt you. Walk right up to it, sir!" and after he has walked up to it say Whoa and allow him to stand by it until it ceases to attract his attention. If you will practice this for the first three or four drives upon every occasion, you will be surprised to see the effect it will have on your colt. After

COLT TRAINING.

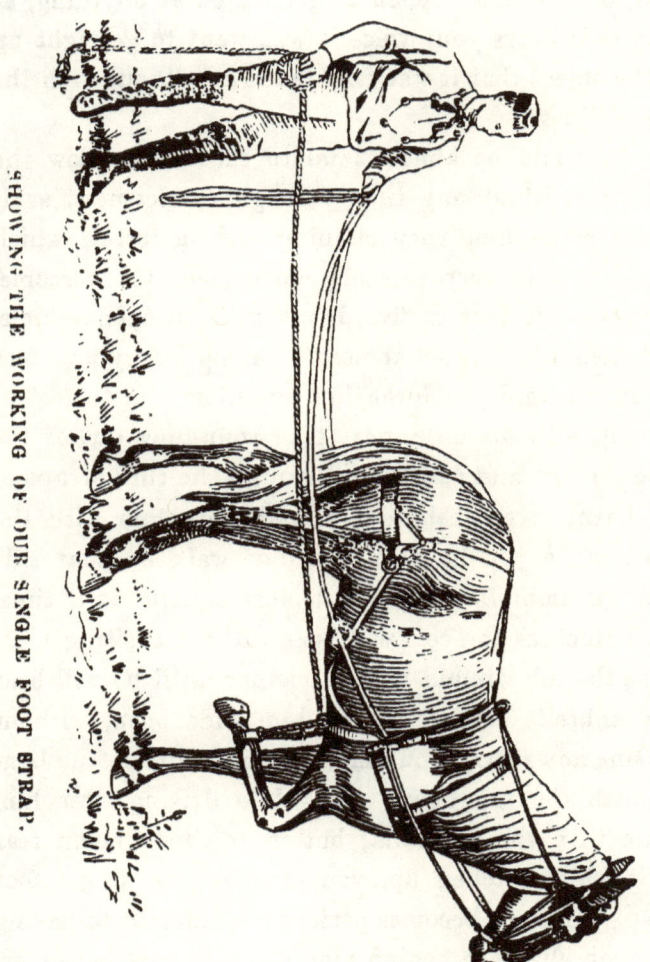

SHOWING THE WORKING OF OUR SINGLE FOOT STRAP.

that, if he would happen to get scared at anything, as soon as it hears your voice it will want to go right up to the object that it was frightened at without even the use of lines.

It would be almost fatal to success to allow the colt to resist at any time through carelessness, as it would make him very cunning and doubtful, which would require very careful management to overcome. Give the colt four or five drives with an open vehicle, and then you can get it used to a top buggy about as follows: before you hitch him up allow him to feel of the top with his nose, next take your lines out of the terete rings and run them through the thill straps of the harness; get behind him and drive him with the lines, while you have an assistant walk by your side with an umbrella, opening it, just a little at a time, or so much as the colt will bear without exciting fear; drive the colt around in this manner until he will bear the umbrella carried behind him wide open, without causing any fear. You may now hitch him to the buggy with the top down, and while driving, test him again with the umbrella; but if he shows much fear of it while hitched up, you can use the single foot strap. After he becomes perfectly indifferent to having the umbrella open behind him, you may next have your assistant raise the top by degrees. You will find that after the umbrella test, he will pay but little attention to the top. We use the umbrella first because it is easier to raise and lower than the top. All of this process should not require more than twenty or thirty minutes when properly done. Once getting your colt accustomed to having the top behind it, all is done, and he will never show any fear of it afterwards. Continue driving and teaching the colt for fifteen or twenty days, one hour per day, and at the expiration of that time you will have all of these early impressions thoroughly fixed upon the brain; so that your colt could stand in the stable a month, or even six months, and it would not forget its education. In fact it would never forget its early training. Early impressions are strong and lasting in the horse as well as in man. Who is there among men that does not well remember things that he was taught while young, and the impressions that were made then are seldom if ever forgotten. It is the same with the horse. No animal has memory equal to that of a horse. Hence the importance of giving him a systematic course of handling. Men as a rule have too little patience in the training of their colts, and they very often expect to accomplish more in a short time than can possibly be performed. Yet it is surprising to see what a short time it requires to educate a colt according to this system, when we measure the time by days. Suppose that in training a colt we were to spend one hour per day, for twenty days, which would be as long as should be needed. Compute the time at ten hours per day, you will find that my whole colt training system amounts to about two days time. You would then have a well trained horse, a colt that would know more, and be more tractable than your ordinary broken horses at the age of six years. There is no farmer or horse raiser that could employ his time more profitably, than to follow this system in educating his colts. It would enhance their value at least thirty or forty dollars, for there is no reasonable person that would not give thirty or forty dollars more for a horse properly trained than for one that was not tractable and safe.

In speaking of the increased commercial value of a properly trained and docile animal, I have mentioned a motive that appeals to all men, good or bad. But to the man of intelligence and moral rectitude, a better and higher motive is to be found in the fact that a horse has a right not only to food and shelter, but to all the comfort consistent with his state of servitude. He has, in the nature of things, to be so much of his life in the harness, that his working hours ought to be made as comfortable as possible. A happy, cheerful beast will do more work and live longer and so be a source of more profit, than the one which suffers not only from over-work, but from harsh words, the frequent crack of the whip and incessant ill-usage with no rewards or encouraging words. Horses like to be talked to, in a good-natured way, and kind words, when in the harness and about their drudgery, will be a better stimulus than the whip; for a great amount of nervous energy is wasted by the state of mind induced by a free use of the lash, aside from the mere physical pain, generally quite unnecessarily inflicted.

"He is often rated as inferior to man, yet he is in many respects superior to the cross-grained, profane, brutal and ignorant men in whose ownership he sometimes falls."

THE WILD, VICIOUS HORSE IS RENDERED PERFECTLY DOCILE AND OBEDIENT BY MY METHOD

SUBJECTION.

CHAPTER II.

All vicious habits and vices have been learned and acquired from previous contests. A colt that breaks its halter, kicks itself loose, or scares you out by fighting, will try it again with increased zeal. He has now learned how to do it. Do not let him begin, but if he should, take it out of him before you stop. You must conquer him or he will conquer you. There is no partnership in the matter; you must be master and yet you must do it by firmness, patience and perseverance. There are no advantages gained by the brutal use of the whip. There are advantages enough to be taken of the colt, which will soon cause him to yield, because he finds himself powerless against you. The first principles involved in managing unruly or vicious horses are to show them that we are master, and to do this we must use coercive treatment in order to subdue them. We have several direct methods of subjection, and also a number of indirect methods. The first method that I shall describe, will be the method of disabling and throwing. To throw a horse, you should have on him a good, strong halter with nose piece coming rather low down on the nose; next, have a surcingle three inches wide, with two rings directly on top of the back; one on the front part of the surcingle, the other on the back part; attach two more rings about five inches lower, to the off side in the same manner. The rings attached to the back part of the surcingle are for the straps attached to the crupper. Take a hitching strap about eight feet long, snap it into the front ring on top of the back, bring the end on off side of the neck through the halter ring, back through ring on off side of back. Next have a leg strap, and strap up near front foot. You then stand on off side of the horse, take hold of the halter with your right hand, and the end of the strap with the left hand. Now you are in the first position to throw the horse.

Draw his head around to his side, take the slack of the strap up with the left hand, and hold strap and halter with right hand. If he is inclined to rear, whirl him around a few times, and press in at his shoulder; he will come down on his knee and go over with a rolling motion on his side. By keeping hold of the end of the strap, you can prevent the horse jumping up; then while holding the strap have your assistant rattle

SUBJECTION.

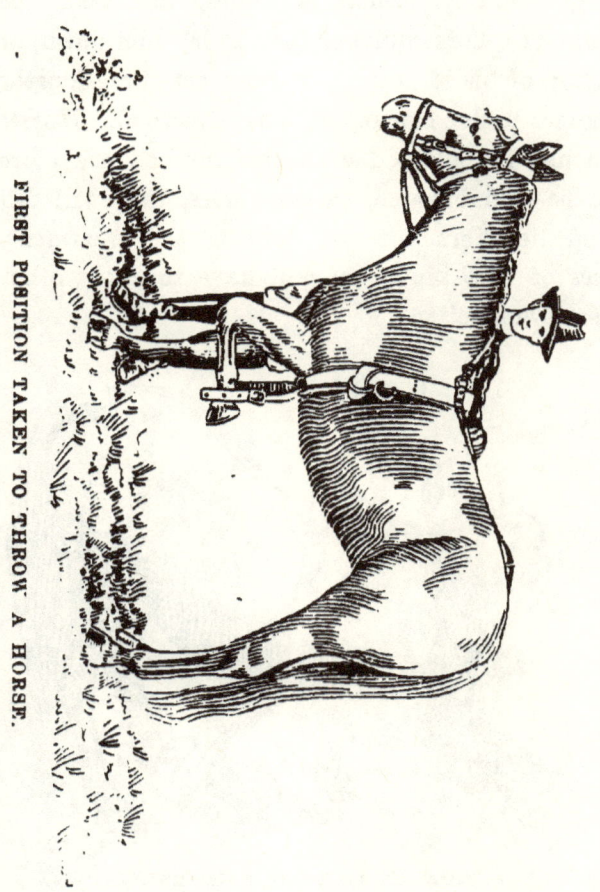

FIRST POSITION TAKEN TO THROW A HORSE.

tin pans, sleigh bells, and all the other rackets that you can get hold of. There is nothing that takes the conceit out of a horse quicker than to lay him down, or deprive him of his strength. We can get three-fourths of the horses under control with this method. Horses that can not be subdued with this method are more likely to be cold blooded, sullen horses, that will fall down and lie there without fighting the treatment. To horses of that kind, you will have to apply other methods of subjection.

SECOND POSITION IN LAYING A HORSE DOWN.

This method is more especially adapted to horses that will resist and fight the treatment hard. If the horse is sensitive about the tail, quarters and feet, take a light pole and touch the quarters and feet while you have him down, until there is no resistance. This will be shown by the muscles becoming relaxed. Then allow him to get up, and repeat the handling or poling until submitted to on his feet. After being thrown to the extent of making him lie down submissively, it will do no good to repeat the treatment. In subduing a horse with this method, the main point is to make the horse work hard; keep him fighting steadily until he gives up the contest. Usually they will give up in from half to three quarters of an hour. After they become submissive it is very important that you treat them with the greatest kindness, in order to fix the impression, and teach them that we are masters; and not only masters, but a kind friend to them. This method is better to be used in connection with other methods of subjection.

The next best way to subdue vicious horses is by the use of the Double Safety Rope. This is undoubtedly the best means of control that has ever been devised, of which the appliances used are few, simple, and easy to manipulate. Have two rings about five inches apart in the bottom of your surcingle, or girth of your harness. Buckle a foot strap with a ring in it around each front leg, below the fetlock joint; then take a half

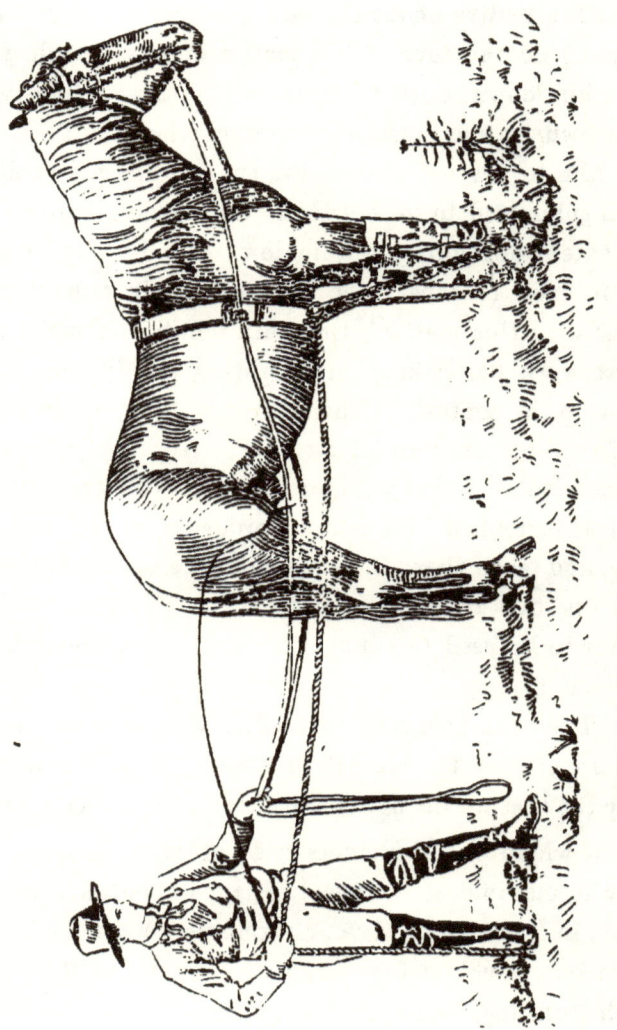

SHOWING PRINCIPLE OF DOUBLE SAFETY ROPE.

inch cotton rope eighteen feet long with a snap in one end. Run the snap through ring in surcingle, down through ring at off front foot, up through other ring in surcingle, down and snap in ring on near foot. This gives you a double purchase upon each front leg. Carry this rope back past the quarters on off side. Have rings low down on surcingle at each side for the lines to pass through, as in colt training. Next take the rope and whip in right hand, and lines in left. Now give him the command to go, and when you are ready for him to stop, say "Whoa," and pull on the Safety Rope at the same time. This will bring him to his knees.

You should always have good knee pads on him, so when you bring him to his knees it will not hurt him. In from thirty to forty minutes you can subdue the most vicious horse with this Double Safety Rope. The next method of subjection that I shall describe, will be pressure on the spinal cord, or passive treatment. It is well known that by hitting a horse at a certain point back of the ear, it is easy to knock him down. At the back part of the head, or just back of the ears, there is about an inch of the spinal cord that is not covered with bone. If a knife would be stuck in at this point sufficiently to penetrate it, it would cause instant death. By bringing gentle, but firm pressure upon this part, you have one of the safest and most reliable

methods known. It is especially fitted to certain dispositions and vices, very often making it easy to subdue horses upon which other methods fail. However it is a method that must be used with great care and judgment. It is our best method for horses bad to shoe, as it can be applied right in the shop. This method formerly consisted of an appliance called a Roll, to be put into the mouth and attached to a strap to go over the top of the head and fasten to a buckle on the near side.

The principle involved, is that the greater the strength of will and power of resistance on the part of the horse, the more pressure should be used and the longer it must be left on. The use of the Roll has now been almost entirely discontinued, since the average horse owner does not care to take the time and patience necessary to properly apply it. The same subjection can be accomplished by an appliance of my own invention which I call my Pulley Breaking Bridle, which is a most useful article in many other instances, and which is fully described elsewhere in this book. Success will now depend upon advantage taken while using this treatment, as it will do but little good to put on pressure and do nothing more. If the horse is nervous and touchy, you should take a pole and bring it against the quarters and sensitive parts, until he will submit to being touched and handled as you please. The main point of observation now should be the expression of the horse's eyes and ears. When he shows unmistakable signs of submission, by coming toward you instead of pulling back, after which the eyes will soften and ears relax, release your power of the bridle at once.

This bridle can be used successfully on unbroken colts in taking any conceit out of them and teaching them to follow you at command. I would not advise much severity in the management of any colt. The less excitement and punishment used in their treatment the better.

I have described several of the best and most direct methods of subjection, and will explain further on how to apply them, and the necessary modifications of the different methods. Next will come a few indirect methods of control. If you have a horse that is afraid of an umbrella, a robe, or other similar object; or one that is bad to shoe or has any similar vice, the use of my Pulley Breaking Bridle is all that is necessary to control it.

While I do not personally approve of the use of cord bridles, except by men of good judgment, yet when they are properly used it is surprising to see what they will do for us in a short time. For that reason I will here give a brief description of a few, noting however, that any result which may be obtained by any of these rope bridles can also be obtained with my Pulley Breaking Bridle.

BRIEF DESCRIPTION OF CORD BRIDLES.

First Form War Bridle. This consists of a piece of hard woven sash cord five sixteenths of an inch thick and fifteen feet long with a knot at each end, and a stationary loop around the neck. The rope is brought down on off side and back through loop. A few pulls with this bridle will make your horse sensible to an easy bit, or make him follow you readily without any restraint on his head.

When there is more power desired, this bridle can be modified by passing the rope over the head just back of the ears, through the mouth, then through the last cord on near side.

Second Form War Bridle. This consists of a rather tight stationary loop around the lower jaw, the cord going thence from off side over the head just back of the ears, down near side and through loop at jaw. This gives power sideways and forwards and is good to teach a colt with sensitive mouth, to follow. The real power is pressure on the spinal cord.

The Excelsior Bridle has a rather loose stationary loop around the lower jaw, the cord brought over the middle of the neck from off side, passed through loop on near side, back over head just back of ears, down through mouth, under upper lip, (above upper jaw) and through the cord above loop. This bridle can be used in controlling a horse afraid of umbrellas, robes, etc., or bad to shoe.

Simple Riding Bridle. This is convenient to use on a horse that is shy of a bridle, and won't allow you to aproach him if you have bridle in your hand. It consists of a small cord eight feet long which can be carried in the pocket. Approach the horse carefully, throw cord across top of the head, bring the ends through the mouth crossing each other, and back to form reins, get on and ride.

The Endless Bridle is a simple device to prevent a horse from throwing his head down and breaking his rein. Little loops are sewed to the cord on each side of the head a little below the ears, and the ends brought through these loops and sewed together. This endless bridle is placed under an ordinary bridle.

Indian Bridle. This is made of an eight foot rope with two half hitches in the middle just large enough to go over the lower jaw, the last under the first, the ends crossed and brought back to the saddle.

THE BEERY PULLEY BREAKING BRIDLE.

This bridle is made of the best three-ply rope, five-sixteenths of an inch thick.

Just a word about my great Pulley Breaking Bridle. There's hardly a habit about a horse or a time in which the use of this bridle will not repay you ten times its cost in the valuable assistance it will be to you.

It forms a most necessary adjunct to my other appliances and it is supposed that every horseman or horse owner who follows my methods and uses my appliance has one of these bridles, the price of which is only 60 cents.

Its use is fully described in my book, and those owning the book will certainly realize the importance and necessity of also owning the bridle. Its use will take the place of about all the other sash cord bridles that are described elsewhere in this book.

This makes us the simplest, most powerful and effective bridle that has ever been devised.

It will conquer more than two-thirds of all the bad habits that horses have, viz: Afraid of paper, umbrellas and robes, bad to curry, bad to harness, bad to lead, biting, crowding you out of the stall, and is a decided improvement over all other devices for blacksmiths to use on horses that are bad to shoe.

The beauty of this bridle is, the bit is made rather large, out of soft, pliable rope so that it will not lacerate the mouth as some other cord bridles will do, especially when they are improperly used. The cord working through the pulley loosens the rope as soon as you stop pulling; consequently you are enabled to use just such severity as the case may demand. If the horse is not very bad, and simply needs to have his attention diverted a little, just a few pulls is all that will be necessary; but if he is a desperate case, you have reserved all the power you desire.

To get full effects from it, you should give quick, short jerks, right in the act of the horse's resistance; as he submits you should cease the pulling and treat him kindly by making gentle movements about him. If he should still show further resistance repeat the dose; then give him a chance to comprehend that the punishment was for his wilful resistance.

Unless you have actually seen this bridle at work or have used it yourself, I will admit that it may be hard for you to BELIEVE that what I CLAIM for it is a FACT.

Yet it is so. Practical experience in the use of this remarkable appliance, both by myself and others, has proven beyond all possibility of doubt, that it is all and more than I claim for it.

With ordinary bridles used for such purposes, the horse would often be very harshly and cruelly handled, and sometimes severely injured, resulting in its disposition being spoiled for life.

The success of my bridle lies in the peculiar action of the rope across the spinal cord just back of horse's ears, where it is not covered with bone, which actually destroys his power of resistance. This is done without injury to the horse, as the effect is gone as soon as the pressure is removed.

This action of the bridle so distracts the attention of the horse from the thing it fears or from its own inclination to disobey you, that the result which you wish to obtain is accomplished in a very short time.

My Submissive Pulley Bridle is the simplest, most effective and powerful one ever invented. Worked by means of rings and a pulley, it combines simplicity, strength and effectiveness in a manner never before equalled.

I have for years been in the horse training and breaking business. In that time I have come across ALL KINDS of horses and learned a great deal regarding them. I have ALWAYS used my great

Pulley Bridle and have always been successful with it. The proper use of this bridle will remove DOZENS of bad habits.

This bridle is made of the very best material and all ready to put on the horse's head, which can be done as quickly as to put on an ordinary halter. On receipt of 60 cents, this bridle will be sent postpaid to any address.

MANNER OF WHIRLING HORSE AROUND.

Another good method of getting a horse under control that is afraid of shafts, or a wild colt that don't want you to ride him, is to take one hand on the bridle and the other one hold of his tail, and whirl him around eight or ten times. He will become so dizzy that he will almost forget he is a horse, and you can handle him with ease. It is sometimes very good for single balkers, as it forces them to move, and they can not tell the difference between going sideways and straight ahead. Hence, when you hitch them up, their ideas are so confused and broken up, that when you ask them to go they will start right off.

KICKING.

CHAPTER III.

I shall first give some of the causes of horses starting in the habit of kicking. Because a horse kicks is no reason to think he is naturally bad or unmanageable. I claim that there is no horse naturally vicious. They are always made that way by bad management or ignorant trainers. Of course, I will admit that some horses inherit to some extent the disposition and even inclination to have the ways of their ancestors. But we should never undertake to break a horse without first taking into consideration his nature, disposition and understanding. For instance, if we have a colt that has been badly bred, has long ears, (hairy inside,) narrow between the eyes, and dished below the eyes, we know that we have a bad dispositioned colt. Now, if we handle it according to its bad disposition, we can get it very nearly on an equal with a good dispositioned horse, all the difference being in the management and training of the colt. Remember it will require much

NICE THING, THIS HAVING TO DODGE FOR YOUR LIFE, ISN'T IT? AFTER MY TREATMENT THE HORSE HAS NO LONGER ANY DESIRE TO KICK.

more patience and thorough work on a horse of this kind.

Nature allows all animals a means of self defense, and it seems she allowed the horse to have its principal means of self defense in its heels. If you are managing a horse and he gets badly excited by some cause, such as having chains or anything else coming in contact with his legs or parts that are unbroken, his first incentive is to use his means of defense, and kick it out of the way. Kicking is a habit that people have more horror and fear of than any other habit that horses acquire. The habit is acquired nine times out of ten through bad management and ignorant breakers. If the horse would have been taught according to my system of Colt Training, he would have no inclination to kick. When a colt is broken as ordinarily done, and goes off all right the first time he is hitched up, it is taken for granted that he has taken all of his education in at one lesson. But should the lines be caught under the tail, or the horse get a glimpse of the top over the blinds, or the cross piece of the shafts would happen to touch him about the legs or quarters, these parts being practically unbroken, it would be quite likely to frighten and excite him as to cause him to go to kicking, and once started, there is an increased inclination to go on until confirmed in the habit. Mak-

18   KICKING.

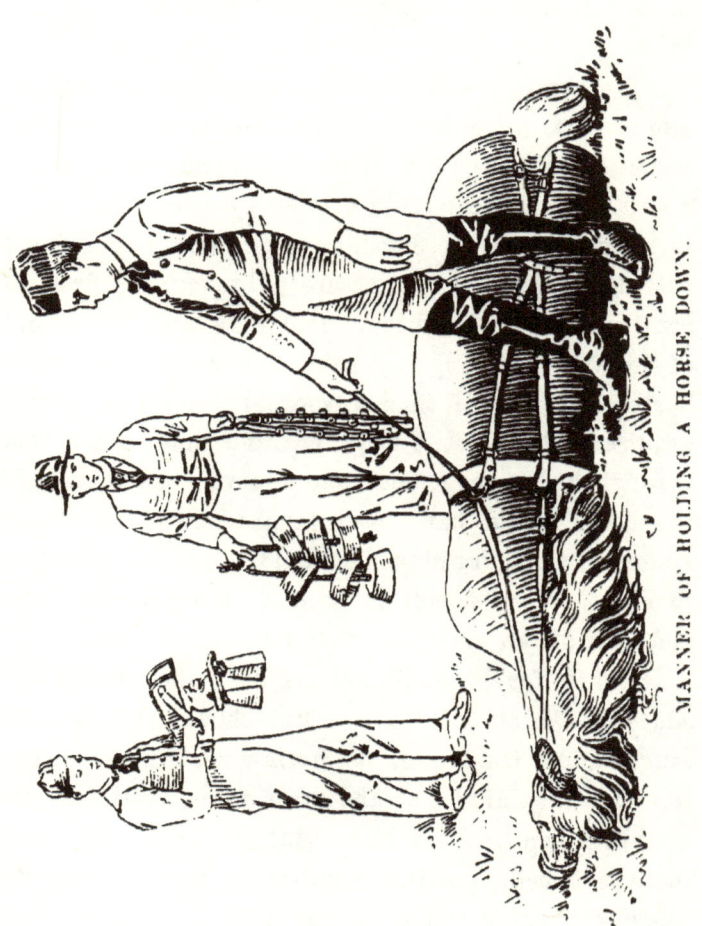

MANNER OF HOLDING A HORSE DOWN.

ing one side or part of the colt or horse gentle and submissive to having anything come in contact with it will give no assurance in having the opposite side, or other parts touched and handled. All members of the body must be made submissive alike. It would only require a very short time to make all members of the body entirely indifferent to such causes of contact by following our poling process explained in Colt Training: beginning at the nose, and rubbing the pole over the mane, back, belly, quarters, and all the sensitive parts of the body, until all the muscles become relaxed. The first thing to be done to break a horse of kicking should be to make a good, reliable foundation before hitching him up, by giving him a complete handling and a thorough course of subjection. The best methods for subduing bad kicking horses are throwing them and the use of the Double Safety Rope. Take the horse on a soddy piece of ground or in a straw yard, and throw him five or six times, according to our way of laying a horse down. Now while he is down, keep hold of the end of the strap and have your attendant throw buffalo robes, umbrellas and flags over him, and rattle tin pans, sleigh bells, beat drums, play horse-fiddles, etc., in fact all the rackets you can scare up. As he attempts to get up pull on the straps, which will roll him back on his side. If he is sensitive about the

50   KICKING.

THE HORSE SUBDUED.

quarters or heels, take a light pole and rub his heels with it, shake tin pans and sleigh bells against his legs and sensitive parts. Show him that he will have to submit. After he submits to all this racket and poling without resisting or trying to get up you can let him on his feet, then put on the Double Safety Rope, as described under Subjection. Take the rope and whip in right hand, the lines in the left; give him the command to "Get up," and give him a stroke with the whip around the hind legs close to the body at the same time; if he kicks in response, pull on the rope and bring him to his knees.

Repeat the command and draw on the rope slightly **and he will move forward. When** you have gone a little way, **say Whoa!** and bring him on his knees and **hold him there** a little while. Then slack the rope and let him up. Next, fasten tin pans and sleigh bells to the crupper; allow them to hang down about to the hock joint, in such a manner as will not hurt him. Now have somebody make all the racket and disturbance possible around him. If he tries to kick, bring him to his knees. Make him fight the Double Safety Rope hard now, until he submits. Show him **you can** master him on his feet as well as on his side. After you have him thoroughly warmed up, and he submits to all of this

52   KICKING.

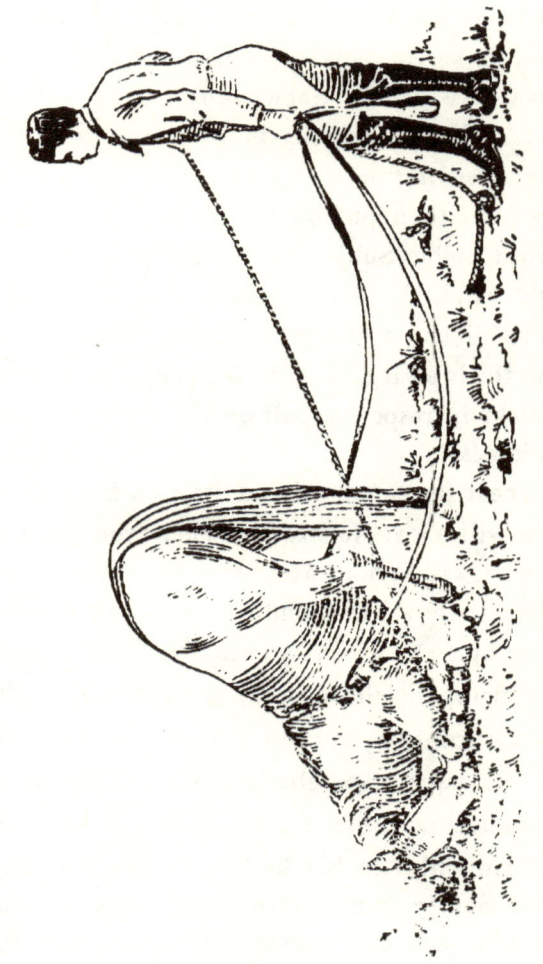

MANNER OF HOLDING A HORSE ON HIS KNEES.

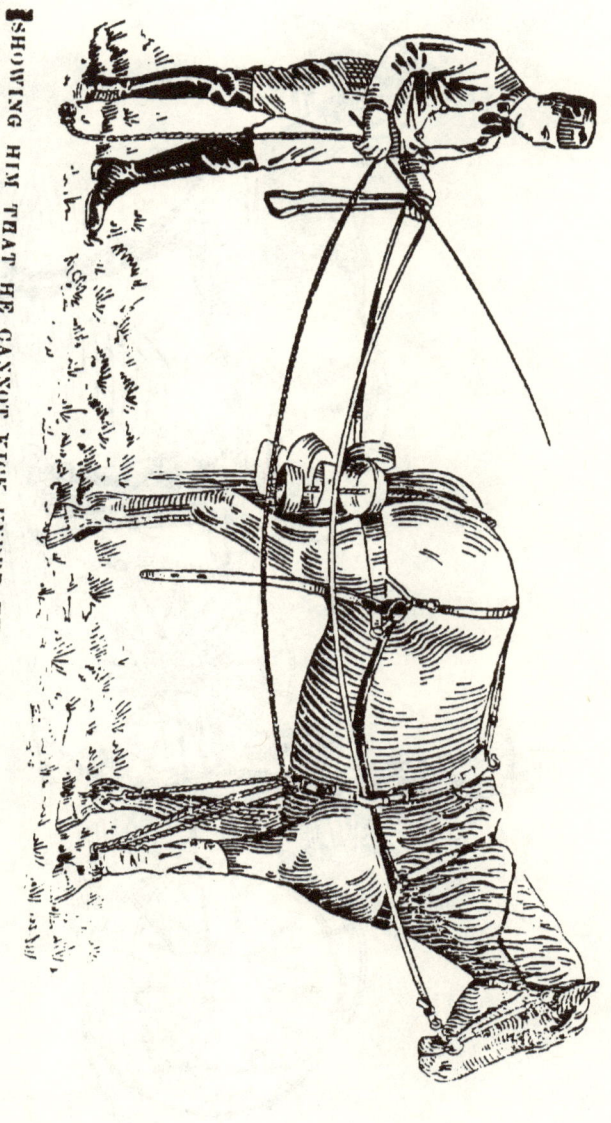

SHOWING HIM THAT HE CANNOT KICK UNDER EXCITEMENT OR ANY KIND OF RACKET

THE LESSON AFTER SUBJECTION.

unconditionally, you should caress him, and treat him kindly until he is cooled off a little; then put him in the stable until the next day. Give him one lesson a day, similar to the one just described, for three or four days, not making the lesson longer than one hour a day. Then you will have thoroughly taught the horse that you are his master, and that things liable to frighten him, or cause kicking, are entirely harmless. In manipulating this Double Safety Rope, always have leggings or knee pads on your horses front legs, and there will be no danger of hurting him. If it is a horse that kicks single, you are now ready to put him in shafts. Put on the Double Safety Rope; by having two rings in the belly band of your harness, you can use the Double Safety Rope with the harness on, as well as with the surcingle; and also apply it after he is hitched up. Before hitching him up, tie the tugs into the breeching rings and run the lines through the shaft bearers, and test him again with the tin pans and sleigh bells hitting his heels, by having them attached to crupper, and driving him around awhile until submissive. Now hitch him up and ask him to go; if he tries to kick, pull on the rope and touch him with the whip, and show him that you can master him in the shafts as well as out.

As soon as he becomes gentle, and is willing to go

all right, take the appliances off and drive him a little while without the rope, and put him away for that day.

My experience has taught me that it requires from twenty to thirty days to educate a bad, confirmed kicker; to fix the impression on the brain so that there will be no inclination to repeat the habit; while you may not need to use coercive, or subjective treatment more than the first four or five lessons, yet it will be absolutely necessary to be on your guard, and not allow him to resist at any time. Be ready with Double Safety Rope to rebuke disobedience, and also be ready with caresses and kind treatment to reward obedience. Possibly the horse will make attempts to resist even after having given it eight or ten lessons, and if you are careless and not on your guard, he will get the advantage of you and go to kicking. If we allow the horse to resist after once forcing submission, it will only make him worse than he was before; because it gives him increased courage and confidence in himself to know that he can resist after treatment, and in that way make his character doubtful and treacherous. Hence the importance of being firm, and not allowing him to resist at all after having been subdued. If you will keep your horse from resisting, according to my system of training for three or four weeks, I will guarantee that he will have but very little inclination to kick, and will bear tests that your supposed gentle horses would not bear; such as driving without hold-back straps, tin pans thumping against his heels, or stopping at word of command so quick that he would almost slide off his hind feet. The first thing you do before breaking a kicker, or any other kind of bad horse, you should ' the blinds off your bridle. I have no use for blinds whatever.

A horse's eyes were made for him to see, therefore let him see; but how can he when he is penned up in a pair of blinders? To illustrate what blinds will do, I will relate a circumstance connected with a very bad kicker that I once broke privately for a man. After I had her thoroughly educated and made perfectly gentle to drive with an open bridle, and she would bear tests that gentle horses, as ordinarily broken, would not bear—when I turned her over to the owner. I warned him particularly not to put blinds on her. I told him to drive her three or four weeks with an open bridle, then, if he was determined to have blinds on her, he should bring her to me and I would hitch her the first time with blinds. He did so. After he had driven her about three weeks, he brought her back and said she was obedient to all the commands that I had taught her, and she was driving perfectly well; but the mare had a Roman shaped head, and he got the idea into his head that his horse was horribly ugly without blinds, and he would like to use her with blinds. Well, I put blinds on her and hitched her up and asked her to go; she didn't even want to start, but she didn't go over two rods until she ran to the side of the road and made such signs of kicking that caused us to get out just in time to save a new buggy. Nothing caused her to want to repeat the old habit except the blinds. However, after I gave her two or three lessons of subjective treatment with the blinds on, she drove with blinds; although he admitted afterwards that she drove better without blinds, than with them. I shall say more and give modifications of treatment, but good judgment and common sense will suggest to you the modifications that might be needed; therefore, I shall not say much more about kickers. If you have a horse that is not confirmed in the habit of kicking, and is very sensitive, high spirited, and kicks principally from fear, it is better not to excite, or get it much heated. About all that is necessary to do is to put on the Excelsior Bridle, get him used to the rattle of the wagon, and overcome the sensitiveness to being touched, by our process of poling a horse. If he is extremely touchy, giving him a few oats, or carressing him will help greatly to make him submissive. No matter how severe the previous treatment, when submissive, kindness will be absolutely necessary in quieting the nervous system. In addition, it tells the horse by his way of reasoning, that the punishment is for kicking, and the reward is for doing right. Some men, whatever their experience, seem to be almost poison to horses; as soon as they get in a horse's presence, the horse seems to be unnerved and excited. They think all that is necessary is to jerk a horse around, to subject him to treatment as if but a mere machine; then if they fail to get him taught anything, they will attribute the whole trouble to the horse as being an exceptionally bad one, while the trouble is with them for not knowing how to reason with a dumb brute.

BAD TO HARNESS.

In training a horse that kicks when the harness is put on: If he is not very bad, simply put on the Beery Pulley Breaking Bridle and use as described on page 40. Then throw the harness on; if he kicks, give him a couple of jerks right and left. Now be careful to jerk him while he is in the act of resisting. Repeat putting it on and off a number of times; as he submits, caress and treat him kindly. Should it be a horse confirmed in the habit, and the War bridle is not sufficient, use the roll, or pressure on the spinal cord. Have the pressure on from fifteen to twenty minutes; put the harness on and off while the roll is on. Repeat the handling until he will submit to have the harness thrown from quite a distance without having any restraint upon him, and he makes no resistance. Three or four lessons ought to break the habit, giving one lesson a day. I may add, that if the harness is heavy or the weather cold, it should not be thrown from too great a distance, nor with too much force.

How to train a horse that is aggressive, and kicks in the stall: In the first place you should have good large stalls. Narrow stalls are always an abomination. They not only make it difficult to get around doubtful horses, but they do not give the horse room to step around, lie down and get up. Put the Pulley Breaking Bridle on him, carry the cord back to the back part of the stall. Do not let him know the bridle is on until you are ready to use it. Come into the stable, take the end of the cord in your hand, and say Get over! If he makes an attempt to kick you out, give him two or three sharp jerks with the cord. Repeat for a few times, going in until he learns that you are master. As he submits, treat him kindly, as that will be very important in teaching the horse that the punishment was for kicking. In order to break both sides of the horse, you must carry the cord back on the opposite side of him and treat it likewise.

KICKING. 61

BAD TO GROOM.

BAD TO GROOM.

How to manage sensitive horses while being groomed. The habit of kicking while being groomed is too often the result of cruel treatment. A sharp curry comb is usually raked recklessly over the legs and belly of a sensitive horse, regardless of the pain it causes him. The horse may bite, kick and almost lie down in his efforts to free himself from the pain; probably he will receive punishment for not standing quietly. How can you expect him to be quiet under such barbarous treatment? Sharp curry combs should never be used on horse's legs or sensitive parts. Always use a good brush on the legs and belly of a horse.

Many horses make no vicious demonstrations, even when suffering greatly, but this is no reason for being careless and rough in grooming them. The pleading look in the eye of a suffering animal ought to compel sympathy from all but the most hardened.

After having become confirmed in the habit of resisting the groom, hold him under constraint until you can convince him that you are not going to scratch the skin off. Put on the Beery Pulley Breaking Bridle and correct as the actions of the horse make necessary. You should never half way control or subdue a horse. Nothing short of unconditional submission will do any good. Always go prepared, and never allow your horse to resist at any point after he has been conquered. Remember, that to break a horse reliably of kicking means that there will be no inclination to kick in any position, no matter how irritated.

THE BALKY HORSE—PERHAPS YOU HAVE SEEN SIMILAR OCCURRENCES. THE MOST STUBBORN BALKY HORSE IS PERMANENTLY CURED BY MY METHODS.

BALKING.

CHAPTER IV.

Horses know nothing about balking until they are forced into it by bad management. When a horse balks, it is generally from some mismanagement, excitement, confusion, or from not knowing how to pull; but seldom from any unwillingness to do all that he understands. High spirited horses are the most liable to balk, and it is because drivers do not properly understand how to manage them. A free horse in a team may be so anxious to start, that when he hears the word he will start with a jump, which will not move the load, but give him so severe a jerk on the shoulders that he will fly back and stop the other horse. The teamster will continue his driving without any cessation and by the time he has the slow horse started again, he will find that the free horse has made another jump, and again flown back. And now he has them both badly balked, and so confused that neither of them know what is the matter or how to start the load. Next will come the slashing and cracking of the whip, and hallooing of the driver, until something is broken, or he is through with his course of treatment. But what a mistake the driver makes by whipping his horse for this act. Reason and common sense should teach him that the horse was willing and anxious to go, but did not know how to start the load. And should he whip him for that? If so, he should whip him again for not knowing how to talk. A man that wants to act with reason should not fly into a passion, but should always think before he strikes. It takes a steady pressure against the collar to move a load, and you cannot expect him to act with a steady determined purpose while you are whipping him. There is hardly one balking horse in five hundred that will pull true from whipping; it is only adding fuel to the fire, and will make him more liable to balk another time. You always see horses that have balked a few times turn their head and look back as soon as they are a little confused. This is because they have been whipped, and are afraid of what is behind them. This is an invariable rule with balky horses, just as much as it is for them to look around at their sides when they have the bots; in either case they are deserving of the same kind of rational treatment.

When your horse balks, is confused, or wants to start quickly, use kind treatment immediately. Caress him kindly, and if he don't understand at once what you want him to do, he will not be so much excited as to jump and do everything wrong through fear. As long as you are calm, and can keep down excitement of the horse, he will soon forget all about it, and learn to pull true. Almost every wrong act the horse makes is from mismanagement, fear or excitement. We must remember when we are dealing with dumb creatures, that it must be very difficult for them to understand our motions, signs and language; we should never get out of patience with them because they don't understand us, nor wonder at their doing things wrong. We should remember that our ways and language are just as foreign and unknown to the horse as any foreign language is to us; and we should try to practice **what we could understand, were we the horse; endeavoring by some simple means to work on his understanding, rather than on the different parts of the body.** Balking is a habit that is acquired, just the same as kicking, halter pulling, shying or any of the other habits; one repetition after another of bad management will soon confirm them in the habit. Then you have one of the most disagreeable vices that we have to contend with. I am often asked whether I can train a balky horse so that he will not repeat the habit. I tell them that it altogether depends upon the man that is going to use the horse. **If the man is not too balky, the horse will have no inclination to repeat the habit.** There are more balky drivers in the country than there are balky horses. I can break a balky horse for myself or anybody else to use, that knows how to use horses. Perhaps the first lesson you give the colt will be to hitch it up, and then too, with blinds on, and say "Get up." The colt never having been taught the meaning of the command, "Get up," will probably stand in its tracks confused, and will not know what to do. You may even apply the whip after it becomes bothered, and it will stand sullenly, or kick in self defense. Now I presume you would say the colt balked. No! there was nothing balked except the man that was handling the colt. Take the colt out of harness; first teach it to have confidence in you; next teach the use of the bit and the command "Get up;" teach it to turn to the right and left, and the true meaning of the word Whoa! according to our system of "Colt Training." Then you will have a colt that has no inclination to balk. As I have given you a few of the many causes for horses balking, and also how to prevent horses from getting confirmed in the habit, I will next give you my course of treatment for a confirmed balker. The balky horse has learned by his past experience and resistance that he can do as he pleases. Hence the first thing we do is to take the conceit out of him, and show him that we are master, by our methods of subjection. I would first throw the horse; if he tries to keep on his feet

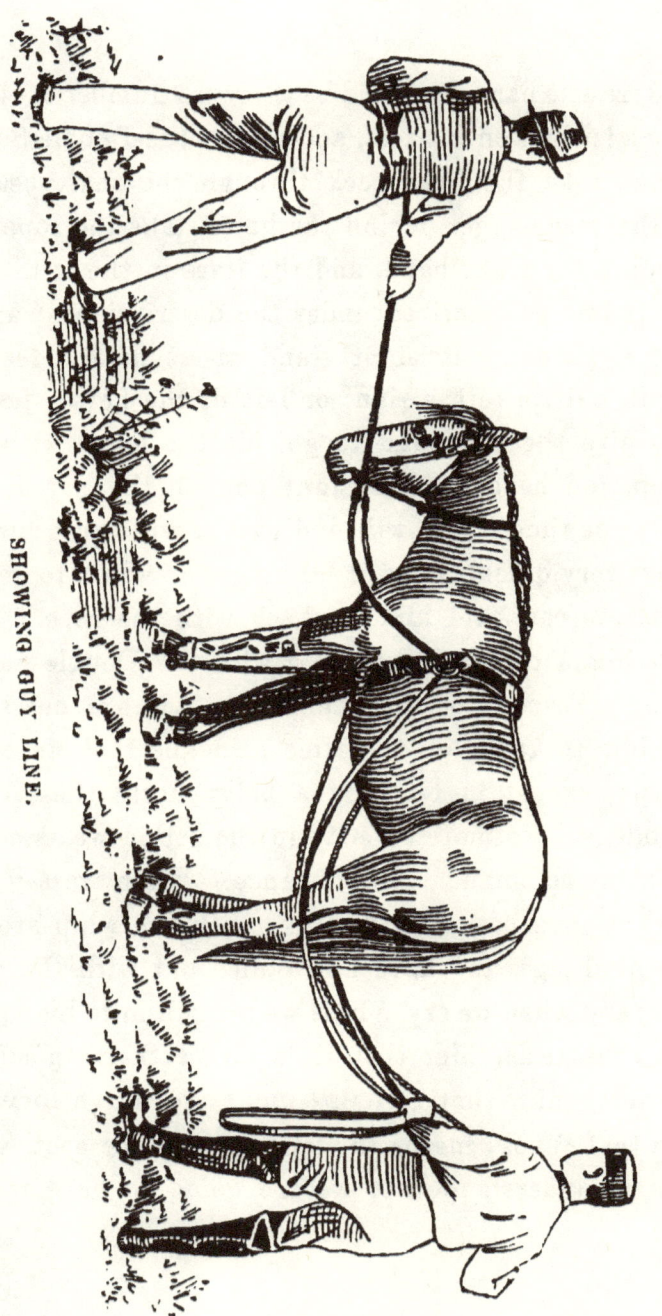

SHOWING GUY LINE.

and resists hard he should be thrown a number of times. Then let him on his feet, and put on the Double Safety Rope; take the lines back through the shaft bearers of the harness, get behind the horse, take the rope and whip in the right hand, and the lines in the left. Use a guy-line as described under the description of appliances; have an assistant stand about fifteen feet in front, a little to the right or left of the horse; just as you give the command to go, hit the horse with the whip, and have your assistant pull on the guy-line at the same time. You will find that it will cause him to move very quickly; and if he lunges or wants to go too fast, you can hold him in check with the rope. Now give him a thorough handling with the Double Safety Rope. Teach him the commands that are necessary for him to know, on the same principle that we teach a colt; except in teaching a balky horse these commands, we use more severity in the action we associate with the command. For instance: When we say Get Up! we give him a hard stroke with the whip around the hind legs, and have him pulled out with the guy-line; and when we say Whoa! we bring him to his knees, We thus teach him that it is no partnership affair; showing him that Get up! means to move forward and that Whoa! means to stop right on the spot. Give him to understand that we are going to have it our own way all the time. As soon as he becomes submissive, and obeys our commands promptly, we caress and treat him kindly for it. Give him one or two lessons of this subjective treatment before you hitch him up.

About the third lesson, if the horse balks from any unwillingness to pull, you should put on the breast collar, and attach a rope or strap to the traces, and bring it around your back, and teach him by degrees to pull your weight. The second lesson, if he obeys all of your commands, and draws your weight behind him, he is ready to hitch to a light vehicle. Now, if he obeys you when he is hitched up, be very gentle with him, so he will not get mad; also caress and reward him for doing right; but if he should fail to move after he is hitched up, give him a repetition of the first lesson, viz: Double Safety Rope, Guy-Line. etc. Don't make your lessons more than about one hour in length, and only one in a day, for the first few lessons. Go prepared for the next fifteen or twenty lessons. Pay strict attention to your horse, and do not allow him to resist for that length of time, and you will have a horse that will be anxious to obey every command that you have taught him. If you never fool him, lie to him, or deceive him, he will never forget your teachings. If you will properly apply the treatment above described, you will be successful in managing three-fourths of the confirmed balkers. To break horses that have only balked a few times, only lots of patience and good common sense are necessary.

Anything that will disconcert a balky horse is a step in the right direction. Remember that a horse can think of but one thing at a time. You can very often start a balky horse by going up to him quietly and lifting his front foot and hammering on it a few times with a little stone. Let the foot down and he will start off all right. The horse would be reminded of being shod; while he is thinking of being shod he is not thinking of balking. Or almost any other little trick that will deter the horse from his purpose will do the work. Sometimes just going to the horse and unbuckling his line, or drop a trace, then hitch them up again, will remind the horse of going to the stable, and he will start when you ask him to go. Taking the blinds off of some balky horses I claim is half of their breaking. Teaching them to have confidence in you, and allowing them to see your movements behind them, will be all that a great many horses need. No doubt you have seen horses as soon as they balk turn their heads around. Possibly the horse has been severely punished while the blinds were on, and whenever he stops, he imagines the driver is going to whip him, and becomes restless, excited and confused. While if the blinds were off, the horse could see that you were calm and didn't intend to hurt him. If your horse will not start under ordinary good management, after you have tried kind teaching and patience to your heart's content, take him out of the shafts, put one hand on the halter, take hold of the tail with the other, and whirl him around until he becomes dizzy. If you get dizzy before the horse does, you can make him whirl himself around. Tie a knot in his tail, divide the hair above the knot and run the halter strap through and tie in a half hitch knot. Bring the horse's head close to his tail. This causes him to run around in a ring. Keep him whirling until he staggers or nearly falls down. Pull the end of the strap and reverse the whirling by tying the head and tail together on the opposite side. Then hitch him up quickly and take the lines, ask him to go, and in the majority of cases he will move right off. This has a controlling effect in two ways. In the first place it confuses a horse's ideas, and breaks up his confidence quicker than any process we can subject him to. It also forces him to move; being deficient in his reasoning faculties, he cannot tell the difference in going sideways and straight ahead. Occasionally this method fails; it is best for single balkers. I will give give you a trick that will be very good for double balkers. You can have it for what it is worth, although I do not practice tricks myself. Take a piece of rope eighteen feet long, make a slip loop around the balky horse's body just in front of the hips, have the slip loop come on the side nearest the other horse; bring the rope forward and fasten it to the collar of the gentle horse; have everything ready; take up the lines and say "Get up." giving the gentle horse a stroke with the whip. As he jumps ahead, the rope tightens around the small of the back and flanks of the balky horse; that causes him to move out of his tracks. By practicing this for a few lessons, you will find that the balky horse will be anxious to start when he hears the command, "Get up!" To be successful in managing a balky horse, you must first control your own temper, keep cool, do not fly into a passion, but have plenty of patience, and you will come out victorious. You will also feel a glow of satisfaction when you have thus obtained a double victory and have not lowered yourself below the dumb beast, but have gained the mastery in a self-respecting way.

SHYING.

CHAPTER V.

I shall first give you some of the causes for horses shying, and also how to prevent them from getting into the habit. I believe in the old saying, "an ounce of prevention is worth a pound of cure." The habit of shying is formed on the same principle that the habit of balking is. I claim that the driver always shies, or gets away from the true principles of horsemanship first. For instance, the driver is driving a nervous, young horse, and he comes to a stone, stump, log, or anything else that the horse does not understand, and gets a little frightened at. The first thing the driver thinks of, is to pull out the whip and score him past; and possibly whip him five minutes after he is past the object; and say, "I'll show you how to get scared." Remember, the horse can think of only one thing at a time.

Now while he is eyeing the stone or log, and you are whipping him, what is it that the horse thinks is hurting him? You would say the whip, but I would say, no! It is the object that he is looking at that inflicts the pain, and the next time you come to the object

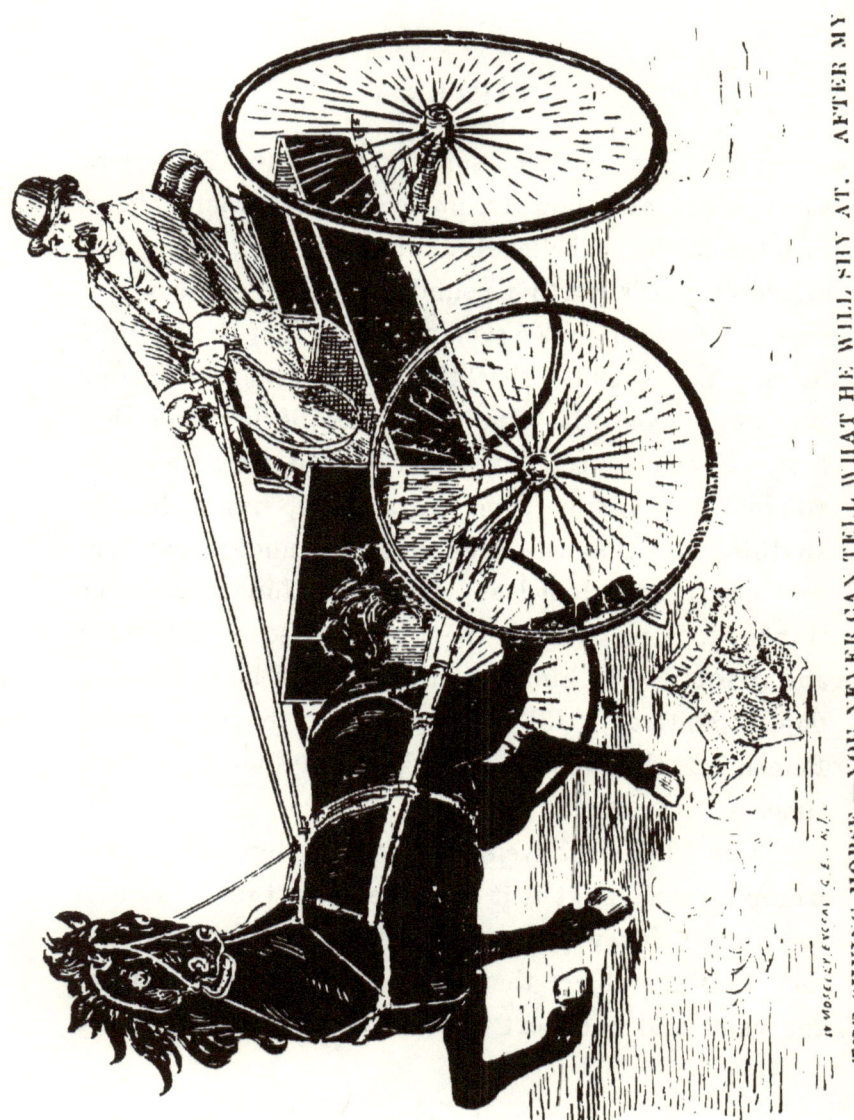

THE SHYING HORSE.—YOU NEVER CAN TELL WHAT HE WILL SHY AT. AFTER MY METHOD OF TREATMENT THE HORSE WILL NOT SHY.

he will be more afraid of it than he was the first time and will try to get farther away from it. A few repetitions of this kind of treatment will make a first class shyer. Or to allow a horse to go around any object that he is afraid of, without having him examine it, and be convinced that it is harmless, will have almost as bad an effect upon the horse as to punish with the whip. This is invariably the way all horses are taught to shy.

Now, when you have a horse that has been taught to shy, or is confirmed in the habit, it is advisable to lay him down a few times, and introduce to him buffalo robes, umbrellas, flags, tin pans, sleigh bells, drums, in fact all the objects and sounds that are liable to frighten horses. After he submits to the treatment while down, then let him on his feet, put on the Double Safety Rope, as described under "Subjection," and convince him that these objects and sounds that are liable to frighten him are perfectly harmless.

Have your assistant hold flags and umbrellas up, and drive the horse under them. Drive him over paper, and right up to the object that he fears most. If he undertakes to shy from them say, Whoa! pull on the rope and bring him to his knees; hold him there a little while; then let him up, and draw on the rope just enough to keep his attention, while you rush him right up to the object, and let him examine and feel it with his nose. After you have thoroughly subdued the horse by the above process, you may take off the rope and drive him over paper and under flags, etc., with the lines only, and treat him kindly until he is cooled off a little; then put him in the stable until next day; give him two lessons before you hitch him up. About the third lesson you may drive him to a vehicle, with the Double Safety Rope on; or if he is under pretty good control, a single foot strap will be sufficient; simply run the end of the rope through ring in girth of harness, down through ring in foot strap, up and snap in ring at girth. This will remind him of the Double Safety Rope, and you can control him about as well with the single foot strap as you could at first with the Double Safety Rope. Now, when your horse sees an object that he is afraid of, speak to him as though you meant business, something like this: Take care! It will not hurt you! Walk right up to it, sir! at the same time giving him a light stroke with the whip. But do not strike him often, unless it is necessary to hold him to his post. As soon as you have driven him up to the object, stop him, get out of the vehicle and caress him; thus teach him that he will not be harmed when he hears your voice and obeys your commands. In leaving an object that your horse is

SHYING. 79

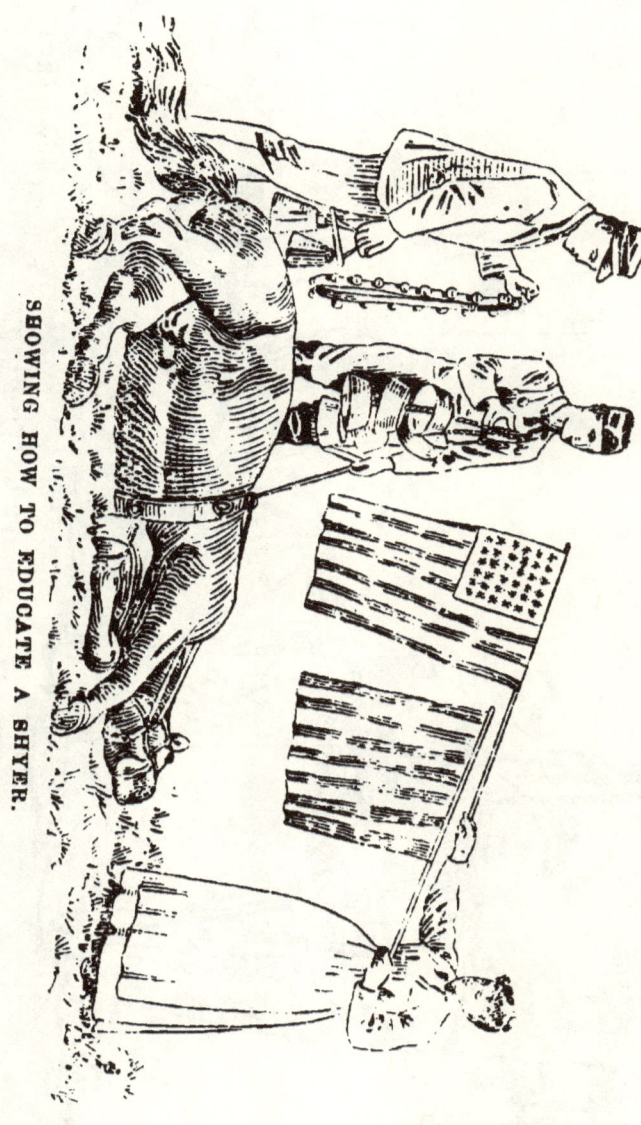

SHOWING HOW TO EDUCATE A SHYER.

CONVINCING THE HORSE THAT THINGS LIABLE TO FRIGHTEN HIM ARE PERFECTLY HARMLESS.

afraid of, you should never allow him to go faster than a walk.

By following the above instructions, in a short time you will have a horse that will go nearer the object that he is afraid of, when he hears your voice, instead of shying away from it. I will call your attention to another error that people almost invariably make when driving shying horses: When the horse shies from an object they will pull the lines nearest the object, while they should always pull the opposite line first. For instance, if your horse shies at something on the near side, you should pull the off line first. By pulling the line nearest the object, you simply pull the head around to one side, and throw the body further away from the object. When you pull the line on the opposite side it throws the body nearer the object, and brings the head and neck straight with the body. You can never control you horse when his head is twisted around to one side. Always try to keep his head and neck in a straight line with his body.

THE RUNAWAY HORSE IS A MENACE TO EVERYTHING AROUND IT. MY METHOD CURES EVEN THE MOST CONFIRMED RUNAWAY.

RUNNING AWAY.

CHAPTER VI.

The habit of running away is nearly always caused by carelessness; but after horses have run away a time or two they are inclined to run at every opportunity until they are confirmed in the habit, and then they will not be safe to drive at all. For after they have once learned to know their strength they will run whenever excited, although you may have the severest bits that are made on them. Our treatment for a bad runaway horse is similar to that given a shyer, except it requires more lessons and more severe treatment. You should take him on a soft piece of ground and throw him several times; then hold him down, and have your helpers to make a racket over and around him. When subduing a horse always be careful that the instruments you use around him will not hurt him; for instance, while he is lying down, and you are rattling tin pans over his head, if he attempts to rise up and strikes his head against the pans, it would have the same effect upon the horse as if it you had struck him purposely. He is not smart enough to know that he hurt himself. The object in making this racket about him is to teach him that it is harmless and will not hurt him. Next let him on his feet, hang tin pans on his tail, and wave flags and umbrellas over him; drill him thoroughly on the words Steady and Whoa! Teach him that when you say Steady, it means to go slow; and when you say Whoa! it means to stop instantly. Of course you must have the Double Safety Rope on. Give him two or three lessons before you hitch him up and make all the racket you can behind him, and make him try to run off. Let him start to run off, and then say Steady, pull on the Safety Rope, and make him go slow; then say Whoa! and bring him to his knees. After you have taught him the words Steady, and Whoa! and he is submissive, you can take off the appliances. But carry the Double Safety Rope with you for a week or ten days and whenever he shows any inclination to run off, get right out and put the rope on again, and make him run. Show him in this way that you can control his running as you please. Keep him under complete subjection for a week, and you will overcome all inclinations to run away. I have handled runaway horses in this way, and tested them so hard that they became gentler while driving them in a run than in a slow gait. As soon as they heard the word Steady, they slackened their pace immediately, and when they heard Whoa! they stopped so quick that they fairly slide on their hind feet. Drivers don't talk to their horses enough; when their horses start to run off they pull on the lines and keep still, while if they would talk to them they could get them quiet before the horse would get the advantage of them. I will give you the best way to stop a runaway horse with a straight bar bit: As soon as you see that he has the advantage of you, and is determined to run off, let him run for ten or fifteen rods; then pull in steady on the lines. Now hold the left hand perfectly still, and give a powerful jerk with the right hand. Give the command Whoa! at the same time, and if you will repeat the jerk and command once, you will invariably stop your horse. It surprises and disconcerts him quicker than any other process you could use with the lines. By the old process of sea-sawing with the lines, you have but little more power over the horse than just pulling on the lines. If the horse has a very blunt, hard mouth, it would be advisable to train the mouth with the First Form War bridle; that will give you friction in the mouth, and you can soon make it flexible to an easy bit. There are more horses taught to pull or lug on the bit by the use of severe bits, than from any other cause. A horse of that kind should be drilled thoroughly on the words Steady and Whoa!

Then use as easy a bit as there is made. A straight bar bit, wound with leather, or a rubber bit would be preferable. Any horse can be educated to drive to an easy bit, and that is the way they should be driven. I know farmers who break their colts with severe bits, and they cannot be used with easy bits, simply because their mouths have been trained and accustomed to severe bits.

BAD TO SHOE.

CHAPTER VII.

The habit of resisting having the feet taken up and submitted to restraint for shoeing is like most other habits to which the horse is subject, caused by ignorant, bad treatment. By a little patience, it is seldom that the most sensitive colt cannot be made to submit the feet to be handled and pounded upon as desired. And once done, it can always be done, unless there is some special cause for disturbance.

There are some horses that are so wild and nervous that they will resist any ordinary good management. When we have horses of this kind, or horses that are old or confirmed in the habit, it will be necessary to use some of our methods of subjection. Our treatment for a horse extremely bad to shoe is as follows:

Put the Pulley Breaking Bridle on the horse as described under Subjection, and while the pressure is on, if his hind feet are bad to shoe, buckle a foot strap with a ring in it around the

THE HORSE THAT IS BAD TO SHOE WILL STAND AS THOUGH ASLEEP AFTER TREATMENT FOR THIS DANGEROUS FAULT.

foot below the fetlock; next tie a knot in the horse's tail; take a rope eight feet long, and make slip loop in one end of it; draw this slip loop around the tail above the knot, and bring the other end through the ring at foot. This gives you a double purchase on the foot. If he is a kicker he will not make many kicks with this appliance on, as the foot would just be carried back on the cord that you hold in your hand; also the pressure and weight of the foot comes directly on the tail. This is the simplest and easiest way of managing a kicking horse or colt, bad to shoe. Pull the foot backwards and forwards at short intervals until it will be given back freely; and when given freedom, it will be rested upon the toe, with the muscles relaxed. Now step to the side of the horse, and pull the foot forward a number of times, until perfectly submissive. Then hammer on the foot a little; after all this is submitted to, you should remove the pressure and continue handling the foot when the pressure is off and the head is free. The other hind foot must be handled in the same way. As mentioned before, making one foot or member of the body gentle and submissive to be handled, will give no assurance that the other parts will be submissive.

Should the horse be bad to shoe in front, put the Pulley Bridle on; you can strap the front foot up to the

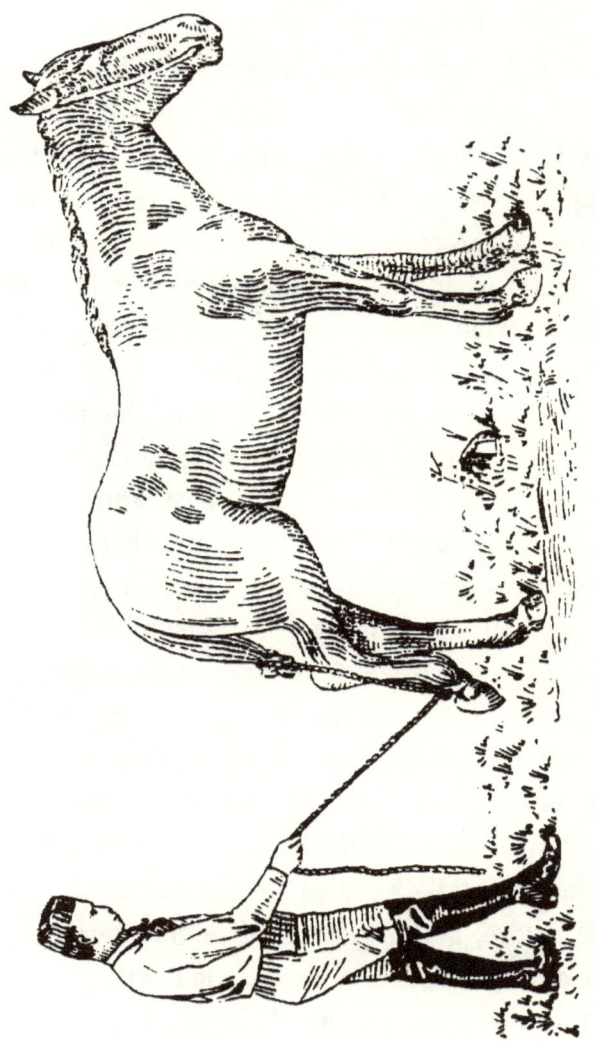

EDUCATING A HORSE BAD TO SHOE.

surcingle or girth of harness, and lead him around a few steps on three legs. As soon as he finds that it is impossible for him to get his foot down, he will give up. Remove the pressure and continue to handle the foot by rubbing the leg and pounding on the foot

How often when in blacksmith shops and livery stables, do we see men go to a horse to take his front foot up by either hammering on the shins or pulling on the fetlock; that is a very bad way to take up the foot. If it is the near front foot that you want taken up, simply put your left hand on the horse's shoulder and press against it a little; this throws the weight of the horse on the opposite side, and the near foot will almost come up of its own accord. How simple, yet how many have ever thought of it. All ordinary cases bad to shoe will submit in from ten to fifteen minutes. Always use the foot strap and rope in connection with this method of subjection.

If you have a horse that is not vicious in his resistance, all that is necessary is to put the First Form War Bridle on, and give him a few pulls to the right and left, or if that is not severe enough, put on the Pulley Bridle, and jerk him a few times with that, and he will submit readily to have his feet handled. I think it is an imposition upon the blacksmiths for farmers to take their colts into a blacksmith's shop and have the smith handle the colt's feet the first time. When first taken to the shop for the purpose of being shod, the hammering and flying of

AS THE FOOT WILL BE RESTED ON THE TOE WHEN SUBMISSIVE.

sparks will greatly excite the colt, so that when you go back to take its foot the noise and sparks will cause it to think that you are going to hurt it; while if the colt's feet had been lifted up and pounded upon before taking it to the shop, you would have no trouble in shoeing him. The majority of colts will

BAD TO SHOE.

AS THE HORSE WILL STAND AFTER TREATMENT.

BAD TO SHOE.

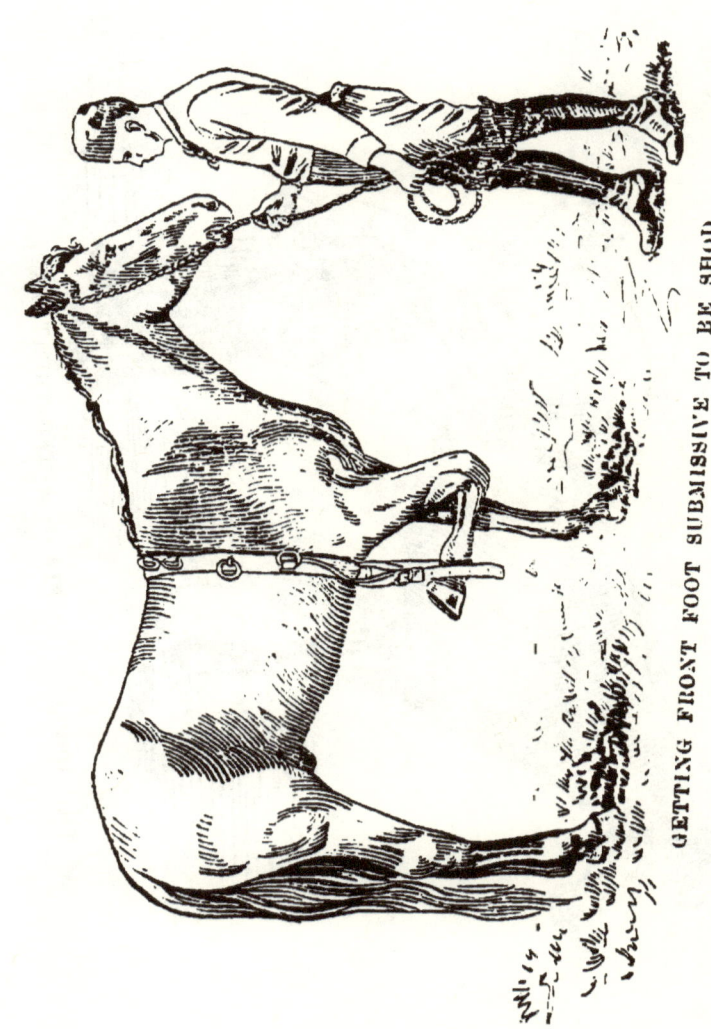

GETTING FRONT FOOT SUBMISSIVE TO BE SHOD.

resist some when you first undertake to handle their feet, but if you can get them to submit to their feet being handled, through gentleness and caresses, it will have just as good an effect on them as if you would have to use coercive or subjective treatment to get them to submit. Should the colt resist too much to handle it in this way, put the Pulley bridle on, pull it right and left a few times, then buckle a foot strap around the hind leg below the fetlock joint; take an ordinary hitching strap and snap one end into the ring in foot strap. Now have your assistant keep the colt's attention with the cord while you take the strap and pull the foot back and forwards until the muscles become relaxed. At first there will usually be great resistance. The horse may kick or pull the foot forwards with all his might. But no matter how much he may resist at first, it will be no indication of failure. Simply keep pulling the foot back at short intervals until there is no resistance. A sure indication of unconditional submission, will be when the foot is given freedom to be rested on the toe. The foot will now be ready to shoe without any further trouble. Treat the opposite foot in the same manner. To give an idea of the power of this treatment when properly applied, I will refer to its effect upon one or two cases that I handled. While instructing a class at Kessler

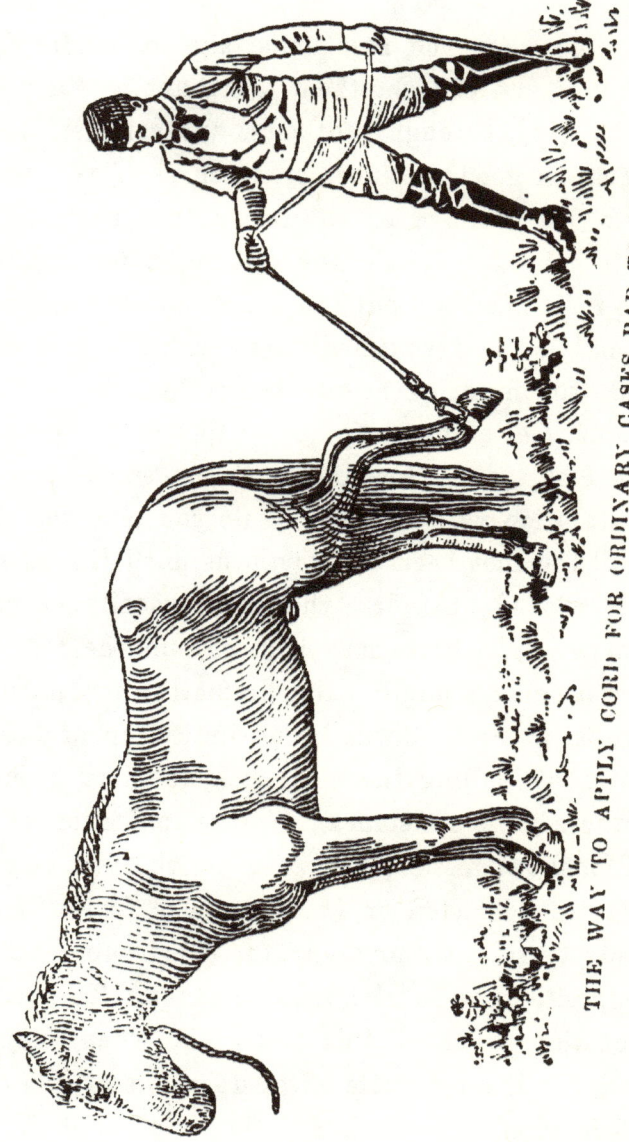

THE WAY TO APPLY CORD FOR ORDINARY CASES BAD TO SHOE.

Station, Ohio, there was an eighteen year old mare brought in to have her feet handled. She had never been shod but two or three times in front, and had never been shod but once behind, and that time she had to be held flat down by six men to have the shoe put on. Since that time she could not be shod at all, and she almost became unmanageable whenever she would come near a blacksmith's shop. I applied the pressure on the spinal cord for about fifteen minutes then removed the roll and put the Excelsior bridle on, and gave her a few pulls with that, after which I could handle her feet with ease. I told the class I would have her shod the next day, and if any body wanted to see her shod they were welcome to do so, but didn't think that there would be but very few out to see her shod. To my surprise nearly seventy-five men came out to see the performance. Some of them came as far as six miles. I gave her a slight repetition of the previous treatment, when she stood right in her tracks to have four shoes put on. Another extremely bad case was an eight year old sorrel horse that was brought to me at Tippecanoe City, O., for the purpose of having his feet handled. This horse as soon as he would get into a shop would commence kicking; before even being touched he would kick the ground behind him with all the force he had. I sup-

BAD TO SHOE.

PULLING THE FOOT FORWARD.

posed that there was something stinging or hurting him, and made a remark to that effect. The blacksmith looked at me and laughed a little, as much as to say "that is the kind of hair-pin he is." The horse had been abused so often in trying to have him shod that he would get vicious without being touched. I applied the roll and in about fifteen minutes I had him convinced that I was not going to tear his leg off, and he stood perfectly quiet to be shod. Some horses will allow the foot to be taken up, but lean over on the blacksmith while it is being held. We treat this habit practically the same as for horses that resist the feet being taken up. Usually a sharp lesson with the Pulley bridle, repeating it every time he attempts to lean over, until he learns to stand without being held up, will be all that will be required. It is advisable to stand at the head while somebody else takes up the foot as if to shoe; just as the horse begins to lean over, give him a jerk with the cord. The point of success is to apply just while in the act of resisting.

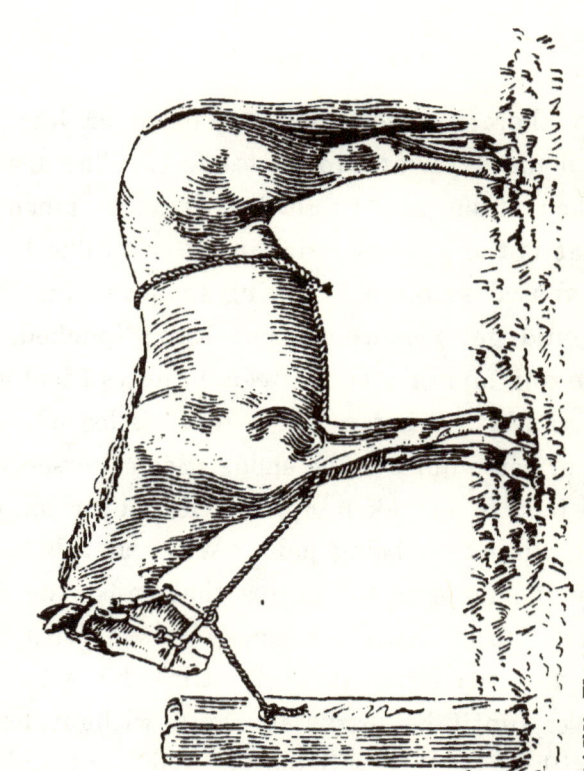

SAFE WAY OF HITCHING A COLT, OR HALTER PULLER.

HALTER PULLING.

CHAPTER VIII.

This is a disagreeable habit that horses very easily acquire when they are not properly hitched the first few times. Once started to breaking straps there is increased inclination to do so until the habit becomes fixed. A horse subject to this habit may stand all right when not excited, but will be ready to almost break his neck in the attempt to pull loose, should a piece of paper or a sudden sound come before him. It is easy enough to hitch a horse so that he cannot get loose, but the difficulty is, in bad cases, to prevent and break up the habit, so there will be no inclination to repeat it. About the only plan that people know for hitching their colts so they cannot get away is, to put on them a heavy halter, so heavy that it would be impossible for them to break it if they were hitched to it with the other end, by the traces. While this will work all right upon some colts, it is a very improper way of hitching, for others. I have known of colts pulling so hard upon halters as to make the neck stiff, deforming and spoiling them, and in some instances killing themselves, by dislocating the neck. The point is to hitch the colt in a way that will induce the least inclination to pull, and when it does pull it cannot get loose, strain or otherwise injure itself.

Take a rope eighteen feet long, (half inch rope that will not stretch much is the best,) make an ordinary slip noose around the colt's body, bring the end between the front legs, up through the halter ring and tie to a strong post or hitching rack. Then make a little racket in front of it and cause it to pull back. It will not any more than get back until it will be up to the rack again. After it has tried it two or three times it will not pull any more, and the more racket you make the closer to the rack it will get. I should have stated in the chapter on Colt Training that this treatment should be applied before hitching the colt up, about the third or fourth lesson. After giving the colt two lessons of this kind it will be safe to hitch on the street with a light strap. While this hitch alone will be sufficient to hold the worst halter puller, yet it will not be sufficient to wholly overcome the habit. To **break** the bad, sullen pullers, or those confirmed in the habit, requires very good management. In the first place, you should have a good, strong halter on the horse, and hitch to a strong hitching rack, where it

HALTER PULLING. 103

AS THE BAD HALTER PULLER WILL STAND AFTER TREATMENT.

will give you ample room to work on the opposite side of the rack. Now bring out your "Horse fiddles," cow bells, tin pans, and sleigh bells, and make all the racket in front of him you can; you may also introduce to him buffalo robes, umbrellas, paper, and flags. The secret of this hitch is that when he pulls, the loop draws so tight around his body that it hurts him so that it is impossible for him to pull long. The harder he pulls, the more it hurts him across the back. But should he be of that sullen disposition that he would set back and pull on the rope without ceasing, it will be necessary to use a little limber lashed whip across the end of his nose. Usually within about four or five strokes Mr. Horse gets tired of pulling, and he will spring into the air and light some place close to the hitching rack. Continue the racket and wave the flag over his head, being very careful not to allow any of the devices which you use to make him pull back, to cause pain. He will probably go back once or twice more; after that he will stay right up to the rack. As soon as he comes up, stop the racket, and caress and treat him kindly. Let him examine the instrument that made the noise, and feel the robes, flags, etc., and be convinced that they are harmless; thus teach him that the correction is for his pulling, and that he is rewarded and treated kindly for standing up to the rack. Give the horse one lesson a day for four or five days and you will have a horse that you cannot make break a tow string. In breaking this habit, it would be almost fatal to success to let the horse feel that he could resist at any point. No possible chances for defeat should be taken. As before explained, in ordinary cases all that is necessary is to hitch in this way, and frighten back a little, at first by whatever excites him, until he refuses to go back, when all inclination to pull is overcome; when in serious cases, a sharp stroke with a whip will be necessary. Always hitch the horse first where he has been in the habit of resisting most, or as near there as possible. You should never hitch him first where you cannot, if necessary, touch him with the whip. When he goes back correct him instantly. When he jumps forward, make a noise, wave flags over his head, or something of the kind, but do not strike him with the whip, or hurt him with the things you make racket with. The horse should be hitched this way at several different places, and he may, when left alone, try to pull again once or twice, but this will only fix the impression the stronger, until he will give up the contest. It does no good to treat a horse just enough to make him stand quietly when not excited or frightened. To overcome all inclination to pull back, he must be handled in such a manner as to make him stand quietly, regardless of any of the usual causes of excitement. Unless this can be done, the horse cannot be trusted to be hitched in the street or any place where exposed to any cause of fear. Sometimes we have horses that will stand all right when hitched by the halter, but will break the bridle every time they are hitched with it. To treat a bridle puller, have what we call a chin strap. A strap about four inches long with a ring in the middle of it, and a snap at each end; snap these snaps into the rings at each side of the bridle bit. Now bring the halter pulling rope through the ring in chin strap. When pulling now, it will keep the bridle on straight, and what little pressure there is on the bridle comes directly on top of the head, without pulling the bit lengthwise through the mouth. Treat the same as halter-pullers. This chin strap is a very good thing to hitch a colt with, until he gets accustomed to being hitched with the bridle, as it will not be aggravated by pulling the bit through the mouth. By following the above instructions, and exercising patience, common sense, and good judgment, you will have no trouble in breaking the worst halter-pullers. We have other remedies for halter-pullers, but none so safe and reliable as the one described, and for that reason I shall not describe any other.

DESCRIPTION OF APPLIANCES.

CHAPTER IX.

Often when I visit a town a second time, the remark is made that Mr.———, a scholar of mine, got his money back quick enough after you left town, handling horses for his neighbors with quite good success.

The same thing applies to you. With my book and my appliances and Submissive Pulley Bridle you can easily correct any fault in your own or your neighbors' horses, and you could often make more than your whole outlay; for their horses are made just that much more valuable, either to themselves or to those to whom they may sell them. It makes SELLING easier and MORE PROFITBLE.

The following occurrence shows the PRACTICAL VALUE of my appliances used in connection with the methods described in this book.

You are at liberty to write to these gentlemen and ascertain for yourself that the facts are just as stated.

Mr. H. C. Blackford, of Eaton, Ohio, one of my former pupils who had been in my class there, says that his having joined my class was the means of his making ONE HUNDRED DOLLARS on one horse.

His son-in-law, Dr. Pryor, had a young horse that accidentally ran away with him, after which it took four men to hitch her up and she again ran away and tore things to pieces.

Dr. Pryor then said he would not hitch her up again under ANY circumstances, and said that Mr. Blackford could have her. Mr. Blackford said that he used my appliances on her, and in TWO OR THREE LESSONS he made her PERFECTLY TRACTABLE, and sold her for One Hundred Dollars.

The VERY METHODS that he used with such splendid success are fully and comprehensively described in this book of mine, and you can be just as successful in other cases as he was in this one, if you own a set of my appliances and read and put into practice the instructions so plainly given in the book.

For years I have been besieged with inquiries in regard to my different appliances. I have previously described them in my book but have decided not to do so in this one, as it has been found that the average harness maker could not make them properly without having the actual harness to go by. And even then it was almost impossible for them to make the Foot Straps so they would not chafe the horse's feet. The Surcingle would frequently be made of poor or unsuitable material, and the Knee Pads could not be made so they would keep their place while bringing a vicious horse to his knees.

For these reasons, I have decided not to attempt to describe them, but to have each appliance made of the right kind of material and in the most approved and scientific manner, after my latest perfected models, and keep them in stock ready to sell at a reasonable price.

I have contracted to have these appliances made in large quantities, so that I am able not only to offer them to you made up more correctly than you would in most cases be able to have them made yourself, but buying them in quantities, I am naturally able to offer them to you at a lower price than it would cost you to have a single set or appliance made up.

I examine all material and appliances before shipping them and I personally guarantee them to be fully satisfactory to every one ordering them.

THE BEERY SURCINGLE.

This surcingle is made of the best of leather, seven feet long, adjustable on both sides so that it can be made to fit a small pony, or be lengthened out to fit a horse weighing over a ton. It is well padded (stuffed with hair) in a manner to shield the back, and also prevents the surcingle from slipping sideways.

Directly on top of surcingle is placed a mounting hold, which is used in riding a fractious colt, or horse of any kind.

It has ten rings substantially sewed on it, that are so arranged as to allow all the other attachments to be quickly snapped into it for the different purposes for which it may be used; such as for the double-safety rope, throwing purposes, bad to shoe and the "quick harness" attachments, etc.

More depends upon your success by having the appliances made correctly than any other one thing. I am prepared to supply all appliances needed in my methods of subduing and training.

Every one who raises colts, or handles horses in any way, needs the following named appliances: Surcingle, foot straps, knee pads, safety rope, halter, guy line and throwing outfit. By addressing me at Pleasant Hill, Ohio, you can obtain a little book, free of charge, which gives a list of all appliances and costs.

THE LEG STRAP

Used in strapping the fore leg up should be made of good leather also. It should be about two inches wide, and about three feet and a half long, with a good, strong keeper on under side from buckle, to put the end of strap through and make a slip loop around the foot below the pastern joint. Lift the foot up, bring the end of strap over surcingle, and buckle.

THE THROWING HALTER

Is made with strong head stall and brow band, with nose piece buckled rather close back of jaw. When this simple rig is on the horse, any boy or amateur can throw him with safety, by taking a cord fifteen feet long, fasten one end to ring on the back, bring down on off side through halter rings back through ring four or five inches to the off side of ring on back; then hold the end of cord in your hand, and stand four or five feet in front of the horse, a little to the off side. Now pull on the cord. This will draw his head to his side, which will throw him off his balance, and bring him over in a rolling motion.

FOOT STRAPS.

The ordinary Foot Straps used to be made large to avoid friction, but this is unnecessary in my improved Foot Straps, which are properly padded, thus avoiding this bulkiness and clumsiness. This shows the desirability, if you use Foot Straps at all, of buying the very best to be had.

These Foot Straps are made adjustable so as to fit both large and small horses—and fit them right, too. They are padded in such a manner as to avoid hurting the horse's feet. They are made to fit on the front feet below the pastern joints and are to be used with the Double Safety Rope. By buckling them around the legs above the knees, they will be applicable for fence jumpers and pawing in the stable, being an effectual remedy for these bad habits.

THE KNEE PADS.

The Knee Pads are ALWAYS of the very best so as to not injure the horse when you bring him to his knees, and they should always be used with the Double Safety Rope.

It has cost me much time and money—more than any other of my appliances—to perfect a Knee Pad that would STAY on the knees and not slip down. In almost every plan invented or devised, by harness men or any one else, the pads would invariably slip down. But I have now succeeded in perfecting a pattern that entirely avoids the annoyance and danger of having the Knee Pads continually slipping down.

They are PROPERLY cupped, padded and shaped in such a manner as to fully protect and STICK right to the knees, no matter what the horse's resistance. This makes a pad that will be flexible to the knee when the leg is bent, and when THESE pads, or protectors, are on your horse, you can bring him on his knees on the pike or very hard ground without bruising his knees. However, it is advisable to bring him on his knees, the first few times, on ground that is free from stones or rubbish, after which he will try very hard to keep on his feet, and if he does come down, it will be without much force.

THE DOUBLE SAFETY ROPE

Is a half inch cotton rope eighteen feet long. There is no rope that will slip through the rings as easily as a cotton one; and on account of its being so pliable, it will wear much longer than any other rope. By having a snap at one end of the rope, it can be put on very quick. First, run the end with snap on through the off ring in surcingle underneath the body, down through off foot strap ring, up through other ring in surcingle, down and snap into ring of near foot strap.

GUY LINE.

 This is an especially strong strap, sixteen feet long, especially used for conquering BALKERS and STUBBORN horses. It is arranged with three rings near the end, which has a snap in it. The snap is taken over the neck and snapped into one of these rings, making a stationary loop around the neck, brought down and made into a half-hitch around the lower jaw.

 This line is to be used in the management of balkers and horses that will not turn to the right or left, or to master them when they have the habit of turning down certain alleys or streets that you don't care to go. An assistant then stands about ten feet in front of the horse, and a little to the right or left, and pulls in unison with the operator of lines and the Double Saftey Rope.

 All that is necessary is to give him a hard pull right in the act of resistance. You will only need to use this Guy Line a few times when used properly, until he will yield readily to the touch of the rein. Frequently we have taken balkers, weighing fifteen hundred pounds, right out of their tracks, eight or ten feet, the first pull.

 There is something powerful about this simple device, that I have never been able to fully explain, yet it is equal to all emergencies.

THE HALTER PULLING ROPE

Should be a very strong half inch rope, eighteen feet long. It should be a pliable rope, yet one that would not stretch much.

THE CHIN STRAP

Is made with a heavy piece of leather, about four inches long, with a ring in the middle, and a good snap sewed into each end of it. This is to be snapped into the bridle rings. For bridle pullers, run the halter pulling rope through ring in chin strap, instead of halter ring. It will also be good to have it attached to bridle, when hitching colts the first time by the bridle; it will pull the same on each side of the bridle, hence will not excite the colt by pulling the bit lengthwise through its mouth.

TO MAKE THE SECOND FORM WAR BRIDLE

I prefer leading a horse by the side of the vehicle for several reasons. When he is behind the vehicle, you have to twist your neck nearly off to see how he is coming on. He will be unable to see the chuck holes, and he will have to come stumbling through them, and possibly bump himself often against the vehicle; when by the side of you he can see where he is stepping, and you can manage him without twisting around in the seat to see him. One man can drive, and lead a horse in this way about as well as if he had only the one horse, for once teaching a horse to lead with this cord, he will never forget t. He will always stay up to his place. In using any of the cord bridles, you should loop the cord over a stick about as large around as your thumb, and four or five inches long, about the distance from the head that it will be most convenient to use, to prevent burning or chafing the hands.

SAFETY LINES.

Put an over check on your horse, with a ring in it just back of ears. Take a cord eighteen feet long, run one end of it through ring in surcingle at one side of the horse, through ring of the bridle bit, back through ring at top of surcingle forward and snap into ring of over check. Next, take another cord the same length, and put on opposite side in the same manner. Step behind and take the cords for lines. You then have a powerful purchase on his head with these lines, which will be good to teach a stubborn horse to stop at word of command. By pulling on these lines the head is elevated straight into the air.

But as I have before said, no more severity should be used than is required in order to secure obedience. When that is done some sign of approval should at once be given.

PROMISCUOUS VICES.

CHAPTER X.

HOW TO PREVENT A HORSE JUMPING FENCES.

Put on him a surcingle with a ring in the bottom of it, and buckle a foot strap around each leg, above the knee. Next take a strap or short rope, fasten one end of it to the ring in off foot strap, bring the other end of it through the ring in surcingle and fasten to ring in foot strap on the near leg. You should have the strap drawn just tight enough so that the horse can walk his natural gait. If it is to be applied on a real bad jumper, it might be necessary to make it a little tighter, so that he cannot take quite full steps. When this simple appliance is on your horse, he can lie down and get up, eat, or do anything but run fast or jump. This is the best, most reliable, and safest remedy that has ever been devised for fence jumpers.

HOW TO PREVENT A HORSE KICKING AGAINST THE SIDE OF THE STALL.

Take a piece of elastic about an inch and a half wide, sew a buckle on one end of it, and buckle around

PROMISCUOUS VICES. 117

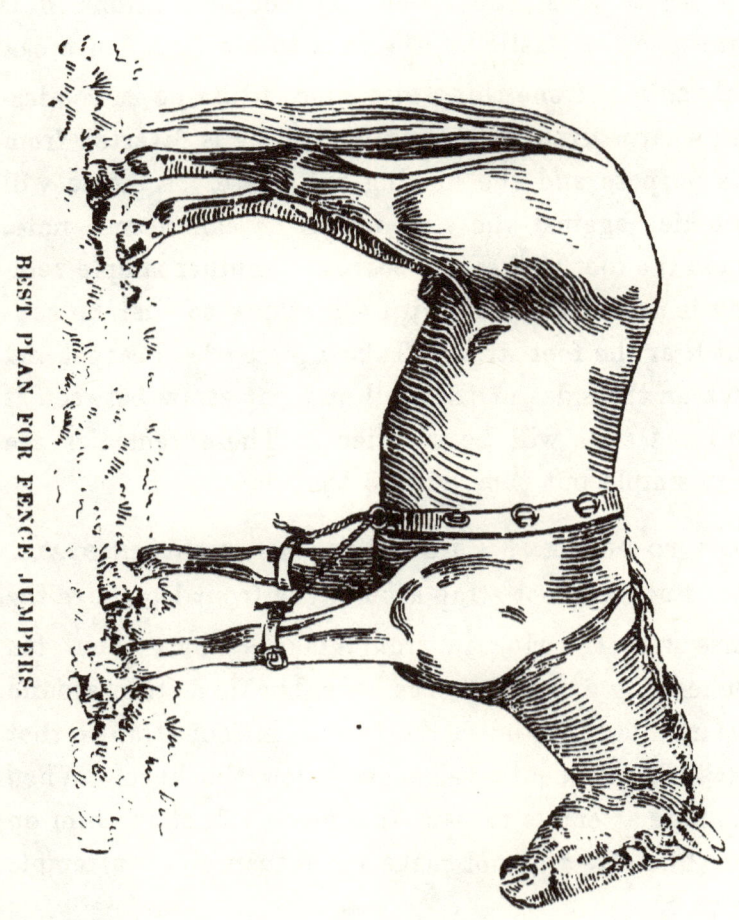

BEST PLAN FOR FENCE JUMPERS.

his leg just above the hock joint. When the horse lifts his leg to kick, the leader expands; his attention is drawn to the elastic and he fails to kick. A horse can only think of one thing at a time; while he is wondering what is drawing around his leg, he is diverted from his purpose and the kicking will cease. A horse will not kick against the stall unless he can hear a noise when the foot strikes the boards. Another simple remedy is to pad the stall with something so that he cannot hear the foot strike. Take a piece of old carpet and tack on the sides of the stall and put straw between it and the stall will be sufficient. These remedies are very simple but they will do the work.

HOW TO PREVENT A HORSE FROM PAWING IN STALL.

Buckle a foot strap around the front leg above the knee with the ring in front: take a block about ten inches long and two inches wide, buckle a strap around the middle of it and fasten to ring in foot strap so that it will hang about five inches below the knee. When the hore attempts to paw, this block will strike him on the shins. He will not make more than a few attempts to paw.

HOW TO PREVENT A HORSE FROM GETTING FAST IN STALL.

This troublesome vice is usually caused by being

PROMISCUOUS VICES. 113

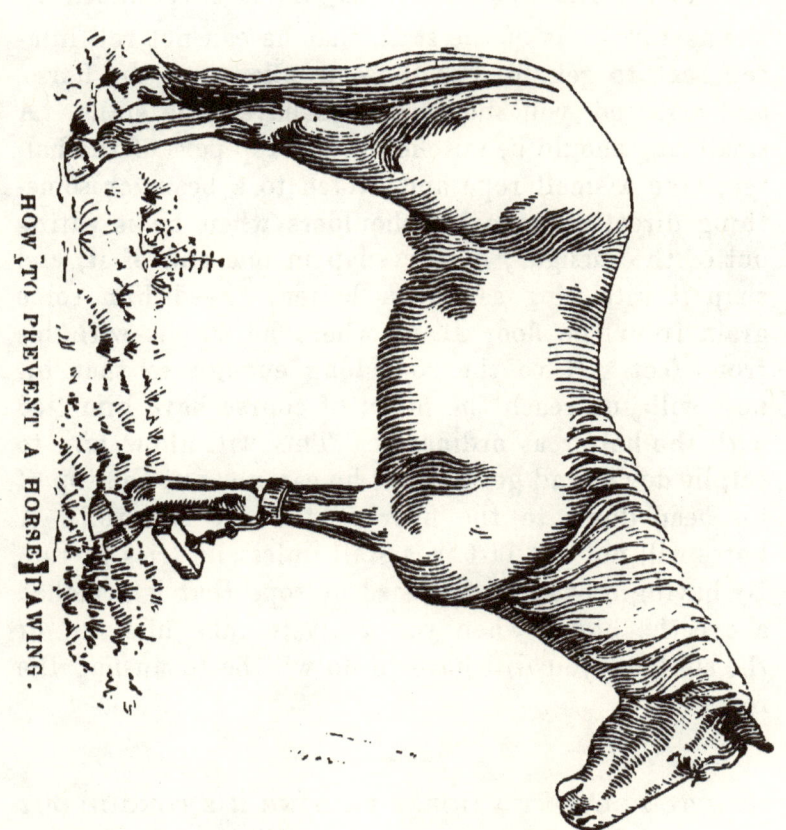

HOW TO PREVENT A HORSE PAWING.

confined in a stall that is too small. When the horse rolls and turns upon his back, he is so cramped by the narrow walls of the stall, that he can not roll himself back to get up. For the convenience of the horse, and man too, you should always have wide stalls. A small ring should be stitched to the top part of the halter; take a small rope and attach to a beam or something directly above his shoulders when he is eating out of the manger; have a snap in one end of it, and snap it into ring sewed in halter. Feed him some grain from the floor about where he stands with his front feet. Have the rope long enough so that his nose will just reach the floor; of course have him tied with the halter as ordinarily. This will allow him to eat, lie down, and get up, but he can not put the top of his head down to the floor so that he can roll. A horse will not get fast in a stall unless he tries to roll. By having a snap in the cord or rope that is attached above the horse, when you want to take him out of the stall, all you will have to do will be to unsnap the rope.

HOW TO PREVENT A HORSE PUTTING HIS TONGUE OUT OF MOUTH OVER THE BIT.

Take a straight bar bit, and file about three inches of the middle of it nearly flat, so that when you sew a piece of sole leather over it, it will not turn. Have the sole leather come straight back in the horse's mouth over the tongue. The leather should be about three

PROMISCUOUS VICES. 121

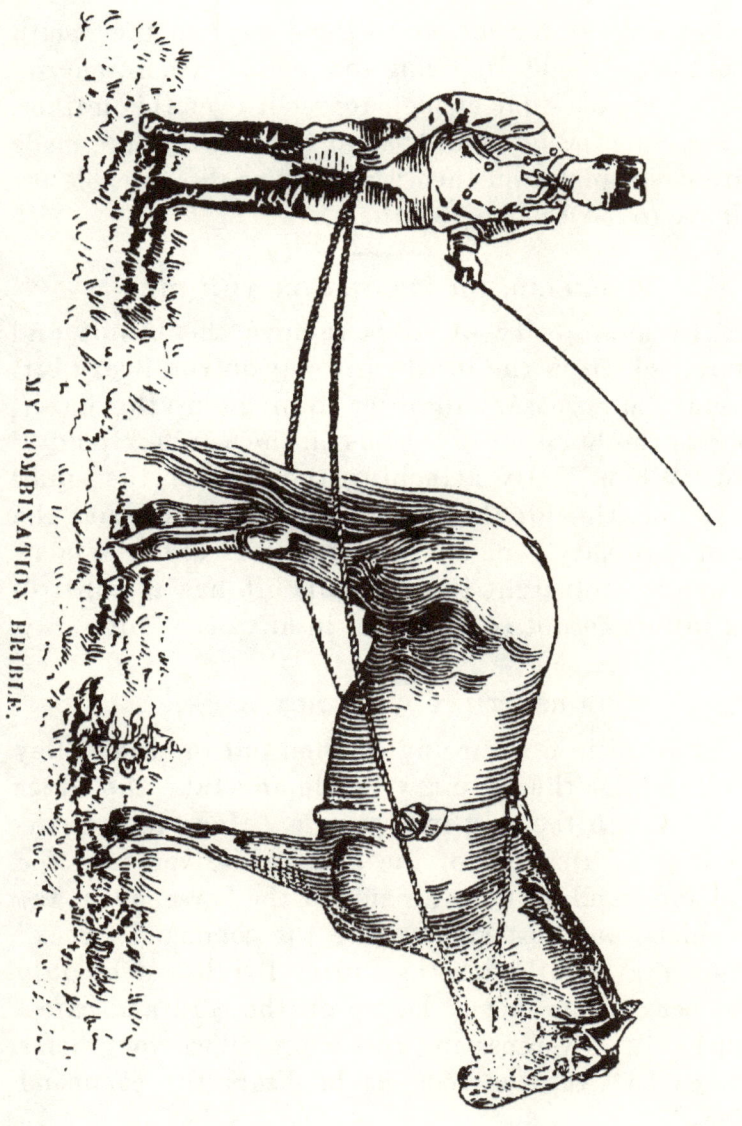

MY COMBINATION BRIDLE.

inches wide at the bit, and extend back in the mouth about three inches, tapering to a point. He cannot get the tongue back far enough to get it over this leather. It is a much better remedy than the bits that are made with metal plates on them; it is not so disagreeable for a horse to have in his mouth.

A PULLER OR LUGGER ON THE BIT.

In a majority of cases remove the blinds and overcheck from the bridle and put on the Beery bit. It may be necessary in order to break up the habit, to give the horse a few lessons on the words "Steady" and "Whoa." By attaching the lines in the small rings of the bit the horse can be taught that the word "Steady" means to go slow, and "Whoa" means to stop right there. This bit has a controling influence not to be found in any other bit.

HORSE THAT WILL NOT BACK.

Put on him a surcingle; then put on the Pulley Bridle under the ordinary bridle and take the lines back through the ring in surcingle. Have your assistant take a firm hold of the lines, while you take the cord and stand on the near side of the horse, about the shoulders, and just as you give the command "Back" give a sharp pull with the Pulley Bridle. If he only goes back a few inches, let up on the cord and caress him for it. By repeating this a few times your horse will go backward as soon as he hears the command "Back."

Another good way of teaching a horse to back will be to put on him a surcingle and my Combination Bridle, made as follows: Take a stout woven sash cord thirty-six feet long, and put the middle of it in the horse's mouth; make an ordinary slip knot, put the foretop through it, and draw the knot tight. Take both ends over the head between the ears; and bring one end down on each side of neck, just back of jowls, twist the ends together three or four times, bring each end forward through cord in mouth, on each side of mouth, take the ends back through rings in surcingle and carry them back behind the horse, for lines. You then have a combination of bridle and lines; you can guide a horse as well with this cord as you could with any bit. Now, to teach him to back, simply bring the lines or ends of the cord, forward, while they are through the rings of the surcingle. Stand in front of him, take a short hold of the lines just in front of his breast. Say Back! and immediately give sharp raking pull with the cords; this will force him back. Repeat until he will step back at command.

TO BREAK THE HABIT OF RUNNING BACKWARDS.

Put on the horse the Double Safety Rope, and tell him to back. After he has backed a few steps, say Whoa! pull on the rope and bring him on his knees. Thus teach him that Whoa! means to stop, whether he is going backwards or forwards. If you will carry the Double Safety Rope with you for a few trips, and

124   PROMISCUOUS VICES.

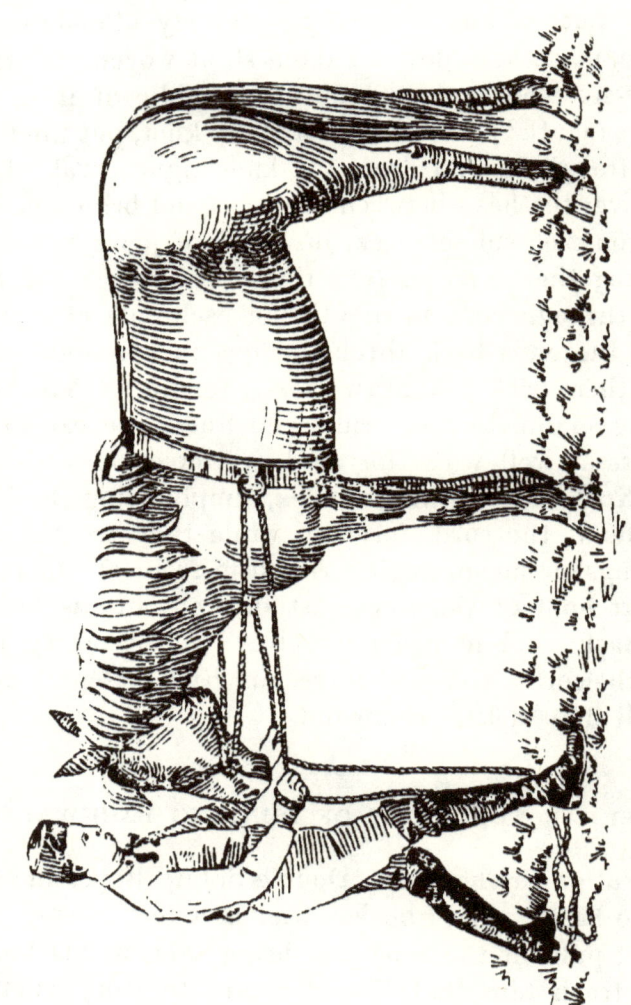

TEACHING HORSE TO BACK WITH CHAMPION BRIDLE

upon every occasion that your horse wants to go backwards, put this rope on and bring him on his knees, you will soon have the habit of runing backwards overcome.

HOW TO BREAK BITERS.

If the horse is not confirmed in the habit, all that is necessary is to put on the Pulley Breaking Bridle and not let him know it is on, and when he makes an attempt to bite, give him a few jerks with the cord. Give him a few lessons of this kind, and that is all that is needed. But if he is an old, confirmed biter, you will have to resort to the following plan: Put on him a surcingle and halter, tie up near front foot and throw him down several times; while he is down give his mouth a thorough handling. Next, put on the Pulley Breaking Bridle; when he attempts to bite, pull him right and left, open his mouth, give him all the opportunity to bite you can, thus show him that you are master, and you are not afraid of him. A very good way to manage bad biting and striking stallions or any other horses that have this habit, is to bluff them with powder. I use a thirty-eight caliber revolver loaded with blank cartridges. When the horse comes toward you, striking or making an attempt to bite, you discharge the revolver in front of him; this bluffs him and causes him to think his vicious act caused the explosion. By doing this a few times you will have him convinced that you are not afraid of him. The horse is a close observer, and the instant you show any fear around a biting horse, that quickly will he take advantage of you. There is not one vicious horse out of fifty that cannot be bluffed by simply standing still until he gets within four or five feet of you, then instantly raise your hand in front of you and hollo, Whoa! He will stop so quick that he will almost fall down. A horse is not like a hog. If you stand in front of a hog and don't give way, it will surely run over you, or under you rather, but a horse will not do this if you will stand your ground; but if you show signs of being afraid of him, by moving backwards or running away from him, it would be very natural for him to know that he had bluffed you instead of you bluffing him. To break a stallion from biting his mate when hitched double, put on him a Second Form War Bridle, carry it back to the wagon, not letting him know that it is on until he is ready to make a pass at the other horse; then give him a powerful jerk with the cord and give him a touch with the whip, and say "Take care, sir," at the same time. The best remedy for an old-confirmed biting stallion is to have him castrated.

When a horse has been frightened by the cars or the steam of an engine, it is a very difficult task to get him over the fright, mainly because you can not control the movements of the train. The simplest and best plan is to treat him to a stationary or road engine first, because it will stay in one position long enough to teach him that the steam will not hurt him. I would first get him under good control by a course of subjective treatment; then put on him the Pulley Breaking Bridle, take the cord in left hand and whip in right hand, and lead him right up to the engine. Have the engineer let off steam by degrees until he will allow himself to be covered with steam. If you can not get him close enough to the engine with this bridle, you may lay him down on a soddy piece of ground and hold him there while the engine is run up by the side of him. Then have him covered up with steam. You can hardly convince a horse that steam is harmless unless you can get him right into it. As he learns and submits to what you want him to, you should caress and treat him kindly. One of the main objects of these lessons is to teach the animal that you are his friend and protector. Get him to have confidence in you, and he will almost go through fire with you. Give your horse one lesson a day for three days, similar to the one just described, then he will be ready to hitch up and drive about steam. It would be advisable to put on the Double Safety Rope the first time or two you drive him about the cars. Remember that one lesson will not be sufficient to educate your horse that the cars are harmless, but if you will have patience enough to give three or four lessons according to the above instructions you will come out victorious.

AFRAID OF SHOOTING CRACKERS.

Lay the horse down and fire off, a number at a time, while he is down, and by degrees throw them out faster until you have whole packs of them going off at once.

Then let him on his feet and put the Double Safety Rope on him, and continue the racket and shooting. If he tries to get away, pull on the rope and bring him to his knees. Give him two or three lessons and he will be perfectly safe to drive on the street on the Fourth of July. In subduing him be very careful not to let any of the shooting crackers burn him, or allow any of the other devices to hurt him. Should the tin pans or sleigh bells hurt him while the crackers are exploding, he would surely think that it was the fire crackers that caused the pain; hence you will lose the very point that you are trying to gain.

BAD TO BRIDLE.

For a horse hard to bridle there is no better remedy than simply to use about half an hour's patience once or twice a day for a day or two, and your horse will begin to want to be bridled. If he is not too vicious you should go into the stall with him and begin at the neck to handle and fondle him. If it is the ears that are sensitive and he don't want to be touched there, work down about the nose first; as his fears subside, work up about the ears, touch them very gently at first, and as he will bear it, stroke them faster and a little more carelessly; then lay your right arm over his neck and press down gradually until his nose is nearly to the ground, all the time keeping his attention with your left hand by stroking his nose and forehead.

Should the horse be extremely bad, you will have to get him under control by one or more of our methods of subjection. Take him out of the stable, catch hold of the tail with your left hand, and the halter with your right, and whirl him around eight or ten times. He will usually stand perfectly quiet; the whirling around in a circle will make him so dizzy that he will not know how to resist. After you are once able to put on the bridle without force, repeat for some time, holding his attention by giving him a little corn. He should be bridled with care for some time,

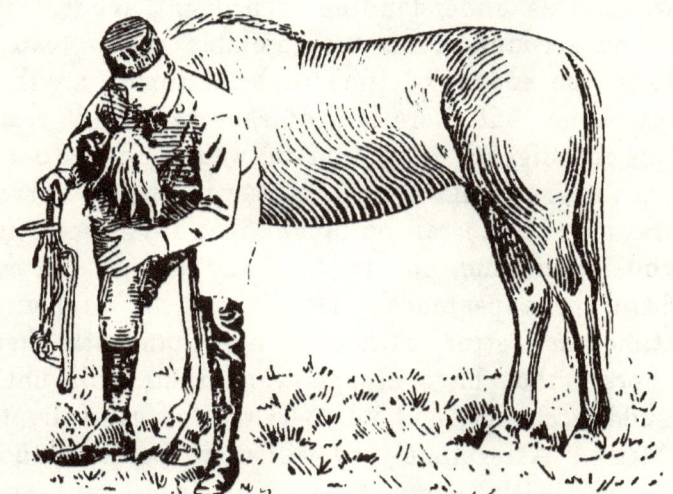

MODE OF TEACHING A HORSE TO BE GENTLE TO BRIDLE.

to overcome all sensitiveness. If you can win a horse's confidence by the first plan, and teach him that you are not going to hurt him, it will have just as good an effect upon him as if you were to use coercive treatment.

BLINDERS.

Blinds are one of the greatest abominations that the horse has ever been pestered with. There is not a man that can give any reason for using blinds on his bridles. All my experience in handling wild and nervous horses proves clearly to me that blinds should never be used, and that the sight of the horse, for many reasons, should not be interfered with in any way. Horses are only afraid of objects they do not understand; and the eye is one of the principal mediums by which this understanding is brought about. The horse, on account of his very amiable nature, can be made in the course of time to bear almost anything in any shape; but there is a quicker process of reaching his intelligence than that of wearing it into him through his skin and bones. However wild or nervous a horse may be, he can be taught in a very short time to understand and not to fear any object, however frightful in appearance. Horses can be broken in less time and better, without blinds than with them; but horses that have always worn them will notice the sudden change, and must be treated carefully the first drive. After that they will drive better without blinds than with them. I have not, in all my experience of handling horses, both wild and nervous, ever used blinds on any of them, and in no case have they ever shied at passing objects. The horse's eye is the life and beauty of the animal as well as the index of all his emotions. It tells the driver, in the most expressive manner, what the horse's feelings are. By it he can tell the first approach of fear in time to meet any difficulty; he can tell if he is happy or sad, hungry or weary. The horse too, when permitted to see, uses his eyes with great judgment. He sees better than we do. He can measure distances with his eyes, better than we can, and if allowed free use of them, would often save himself by the quickness of sight from collisions, when the driver would fail to do so by a timely pull of the lines. It would also save many accidents to pedestrians in the streets, as no horse will run over a person he can see. Blinds are an unnecessary and injurious incumbrance. If you will take the time to notice all the horses that go along the street for an hour, or notice all the bridles on horses in a funeral procession, some day, you will not find one pair of blinds out of three that are adjusted right. Some of them will be too high or too low, some will have one side flapping straight out, while the other side will be pinched tight up against the eye; others will have the corners of the blinds bent and sticking towards the eye, sometimes in them, keeping the horse continually batting his eyes. I have seen a number of blinds pinched in so tight against the eyes that the horse could not see at all. Now, after your observation convinces you that two-thirds of the blinds that are used are adjusted in about the manner described, you will have to agree with me when I say that blinds are a cruelty to **animals**. I think there ought to be a law passed prohibiting the use of them. However, I am glad to know that people are beginning to see the absurdity of them, and in a few years hence they will be a thing to be read of as one of the follies happily reformed.

WILL NOT STAND.

The first thing take off the blinds and give the horse a chance to see your movements; then teach him that Whoa! means to stand, and not move until told, in the following manner: Put on the Double Safety Rope; pass the lines through the side rings of the surcingle, or shaft bearers of the harness. Then crack the whip, wave flags over him, and make all the racket you can around him. If he starts, say Whoa! and bring him on his knees. Give him one or two lessons of this kind before you hitch him up; then give him a few lessons while hitched up. If it is a colt that you want to teach to stand, take it into an inclosure, stand it in the middle of it, commence at the shoulder to walk around it, keeping as close to it as possible, keeping its attention by caressing it, and by degrees make your circles a little larger, and walk a little faster. Watch the colt's eyes and ears very closely. Should he attempt to move, pick up the lines, say Whoa! and give him a raking pull with the lines; then immediately slack them. Keep him as near as possible on one spot and he will get your idea sooner than to allow him to change positions so often. After he once understands that you intend to have him stand until you ask him to go, you can then stand him in another place and proceed as before. You should not teach him more than half an hour at a time.

THE WORKING OF THE DOUBLE SAFETY ROPE, SHOWING ONE FOOT UP.

AFRAID OF UMBRELLA.

Put on him the Pulley Breaking Bridle, which will hold any horse wherever you want him.

Now present the umbrella closed and let him feel it with his nose; then open partially, and let him thoroughly examine it. If he should make an effort to get away, give him a few pulls with the bridle. You may now open the umbrella wide, and stand in front of the horse, or a little to the near side, holding the cord in left hand; throw your right arm over the left, and hold the umbrella in your right hand, directly in front of the horse. Now hold his attention by giving little short jerks with the cord, while you swing the umbrella up high and bring it down over his head with a quick motion, and hold him right under it. Lead him around under it for a little while; then open and shut it, and let him feel it with his "fingers."

Now have your assistant go off some distance, and approach slowly from different directions, and hold it over his head. If at any point there is much fear shown, close it, and let the horse examine it again; then repeat, until it can be brought up in any manner, while swinging it, without attracting notice. Two lessons will be enough to teach ordinary cases not to have any fear of an umbrella.

FEAR OF ROBE.

That practically the same as for a horse afraid of *[illegible]* If the horse is so determined in his resistance, it would be advisable to put on him the Pulley Breaking Bridle; then present the robe, at first having it folded, and just allow him to see and feel of one corner of it. By degrees unfold it, and let him see the whole of the robe; if he tries to get away from it let him feel the power you have over him with the cord. Then hold his attention with the cord until you get the robe close to his head, when you throw the robe over his head, leaving it completely covered for a short time, and then rub it over his body. Place it in different positions about him, and it will only be a short time until he will be perfectly indifferent to a robe. In some cases it might be necessary to throw the horse down, and present the robe while he is down, and commence at the head to get him used to it, by letting him feel and smell it, and rub his mane, neck and body with it, until he is convinced the robe is harmless. Then let him on his feet, and continue operations until you can throw it on him at a distance of eight or ten feet without exciting fear. Both sides must be treated alike. To overcome all fear of the robe, it will be better to repeat the lesson several times.

AFRAID OF THE SOUND OF A GUN.

If your horse is afraid of the sound of a gun, put on him the Pulley Breaking Bridle. Have some one to take a gun and snap caps some distance from him, gradually going nearer, and repeating until it can be done over his body. Then have him go farther from

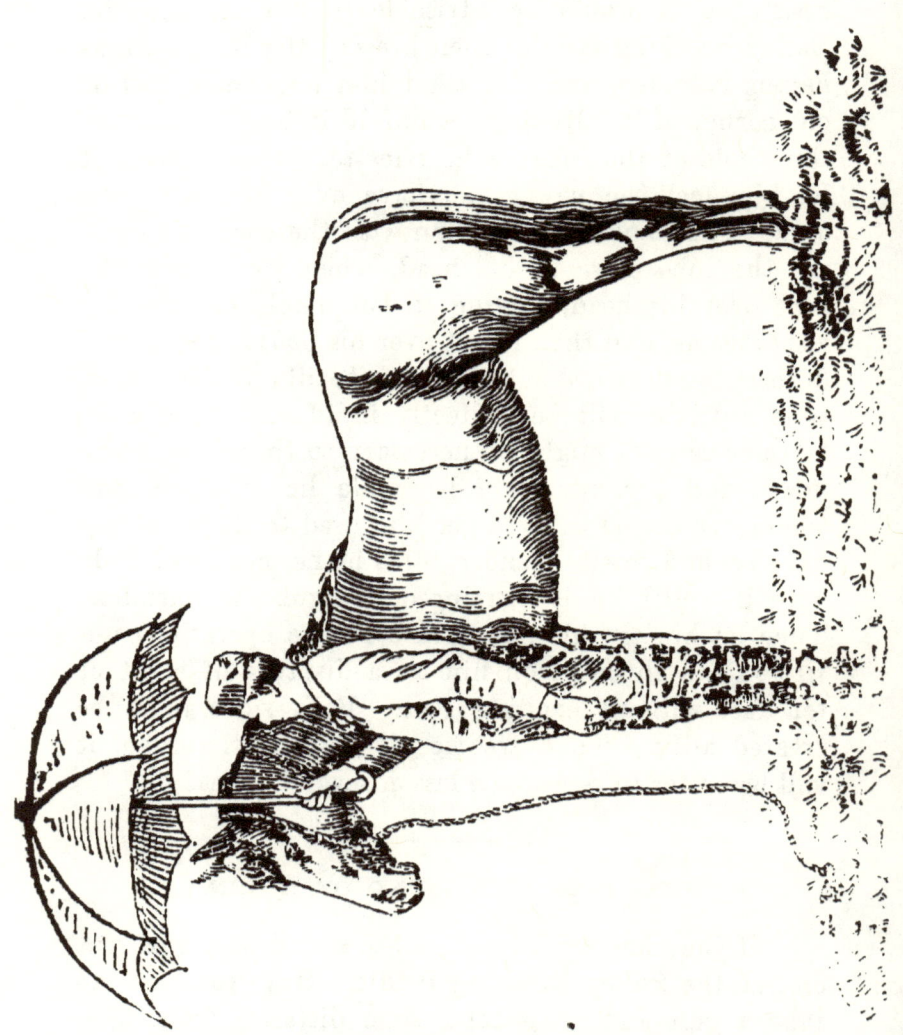

OPENING THE UMBRELLA OVER THE HEAD.

PROMISCUOUS VICES.

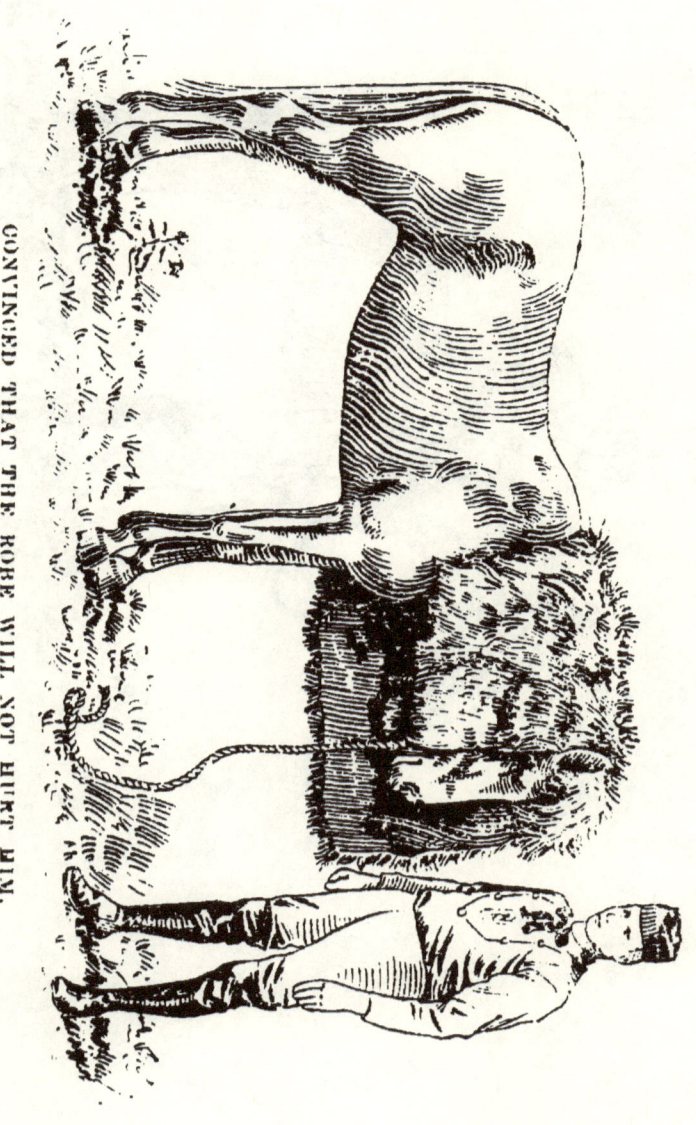

CONVINCED THAT THE ROBE WILL NOT HURT HIM.

AS THE HORSE WILL STAND AFTER THE PREVIOUS TREATMENT.

the horse again, and commence firing with small charge of powder; increase the charge until he will allow a full charge to be fired near him. After you have given him three or four lessons of this kind, you will be surprised to see how indifferent he will be to any sudden sounds that otherwise might frighten him.

AFRAID OF HOGS AND DOGS.

Put on the Double Safety Rope; run the lines back through the shaft bearers of the harness, and take him in a large lot where there are hogs; if he tries to get away from them bring him on his knees with the rope. Then make him get after the hogs and run them all over the lot, and it will be but a short time until he will be convinced that the hogs will not hurt him, and will pay no attention to them. Usually horses that are afraid of hogs are afraid of dogs too, and by teaching them not to be afraid of hogs they will not be afraid of dogs.

HOW TO PREVENT A HORSE SWITCHING HIS TAIL.

Take a piece of leather four or five inches wide, about as long as the tail bone of the horse, and attach a crupper to one end of it. Have a pocket sewed on this leather large enough to hold about three pounds of shot, also sew two or three small straps and buckles on it. Now fill this pocket with shot, and buckle it to the back strap of your harness, instead of the ordinary crupper, and buckle the small straps around the bone of the horse's tail. By this means the appliance cannot be seen, and it will be impossible for the horse to switch his tail when this appliance is on. By using this for a few weeks you will overcome the habit of tail switching.

THE OVER CHECK AND CURB-BIT.

CHAPTER XI.

I am as radically opposed to this appliance as I am to blinds on the bridle. If you have a horse that was born without style, you might as well submit at once to let him go through life for what he is worth without torturing him, because there is no art of man that can add style to him if it is not natural for him to have style. But man can destroy style and natural beauty by the use of straps and rigging. I have seen horses that were naturally stylish, having the natural curve in their neck, with all the beauty that nature could give them, and then have it all dstroyed by the use of the overdraw check rein. This straight strap is not only a disfigurement of itself, but it destroys the appearance of the horse by taking the curve out of the horse's neck and converting it into a straight line; it also wears off its mane, but the rein coming from the nose directly over the horse's head, lifts his nose up almost straight with his ears, turns the eyes upwards and causes the neck to appear a great deal smaller than it really is, thus destroying the style and handsome appearance of a fine horse. Horses look handsomer when driven with open bridles and no check reins.

They can travel easier and more gracefully when allowed the free use of their head and sight, than any other way you could manage them. You can more fully realize the absurdity of using this appliance if you will notice the horses while hitched in the streets that have the overdraw check reins on. You will see them paw the ground, champing the bit, or turning the head to one side in order to loosen the check. This is certainly cruel. You should always use the side reins, and then not draw the head higher than his natural way of carrying it. In all my practice of handling kickers and all kinds of nervous, high strung horses, I give them their first training without any rein at all, allowing them free use of their head and neck, and then I rein them very slack, simply to prevent them putting their heads to the ground when we stop them. It is a rank barbarity, and a serious impediment to any horse. It causes roaring, poll evil, paralysis of the shoulders and bowed knees. The overdraw check should be prohibited by law. The great horseman, Rarey, says: "The bitting bridle, as used, is one of the very worst cruelties."

If used at all, it should never be used when tight, more than fifteen minutes at a time. I have seen colts permanently injured by it.

I am aware that many horsemen differ from me on this subject, but I speak from experience and close observation. For the sake of those who may dispute my position in this regard, I adduce further evidence in the shape of facts and opinions of undoubted authority.

"The Chicago Times," in a recent article in which it joins the ministers and the other good people in a vigorous protest against a proposition to establish Sunday horse-racing in that city, takes occasion to administer stinging rebuke where it is much needed:

"And, by the way, while the ministers are about the good work of suppressing Sunday horse-races, a little attention to an atrocity that comes nearer their own doors, or the doors of their churches, might not be amiss. Waiting in front of almost every church every Sunday may be seen handsome carriages, the horses attached to which have their heads drawn out to nearly a straight line with their necks by an invention of the devil called an 'over-check rein.' The poor brutes sometimes endure this constrained and unnatural position for hours."

"Said a noted eastern preacher once: 'I have little faith in the religion of a man whose horse does not know he is a Christian.' It is time for preachers to do something in the way of impressing this gospel of decent humanity to animals upon their hearers."

The late Sir Arthur Helps said: "Whenever I see horses suffering from a tight check-rein, I know the owner is unobservant, cruel or pompous. He is unobservant or he would see that his horses are suffering. He is ignorant or he would know that a horse loses much of his power of pulling and cannot recover himself if he stumbles; and he is cruel if,—observing and knowing, he does not remedy it. He is pompous and vulgar if he prefers that his horses rear their heads on high and rattle their trappings, to being dealt with humanely and reasonably. When I look at the coat-of-arms on these carriages I know who are the greatest fools in London in the upper classes. The idiot and brute of a coachman likes to sit behind these poor, tortured, faithful martyrs, with their tied up heads, but his master ought to know better."

H. W. Herbert, in his "Hints to Horse Keepers," says: "The check, or bearing rein, is an unaccountable mistake in the harness invention. While it holds the horse's head in an unnatural, ungraceful and uncomfortable position, it gives the mouth a callous, horny character, and entirely destroys all chance for fine driving. The check rein is considered valuable to prevent horses from grazing or lowering the head. The same end may be equally attained by substituting a simple bridle-rein, fastened to the saddle without passing through the loops of the throatlatch."

Another writer says:

"Tying one part of an animal's body to another does not necessarily keep him on his feet. It is the pull from the arm of the driver that makes the horse regain himself when he stumbles. One might as well say that tying a man's head back to a belt at his waist would prevent him from falling if he stumbled in a race."

Over five hundred Veterinary Surgeons have signed a paper condemning tight check-reins, as painful to horses and productive of disease, causing distortion of the windpipe to such a degree as to impede respiration. They mention paralysis of the muscles of the face, megrims, apoplexy, coma, and inflammation as some of the results of its use.

The over-check rein will often cause a horse to become knee-sprung. It destroys the delicate sensitiveness to the bit which is most desirable in guiding a horse.

Dr. Kitching says: "If a horse pulling a load has his head held in by a check-rein, he cannot throw his weight into his collar, and is hindered from giving his body that position which is the most natural and effective." He goes on to speak of the consequent strain of his limbs and muscles, and the injury caused by the constrained position of the head, whereby the breathing and circulation are affected, and the horse made restless, irritable, and uncomfortable. He says: "The check-rein inflicts unceasing torture upon the animal in another way. By holding the head upward, it puts the muscles of the neck on a constant strain. They become painfully uneasy and tired. If the horse cannot bear it, he rests the weight of his head upon the rein, and his mouth is violently stretched. Thus, he only exchanges one torture for another. To sum up in a word, the check-rein lessens the horse's strength; brings on disease; keeps him in pain; frets and injures his mouth; and spoils his temper."

I am glad to help in giving publicity to the following object lesson, and wish it might help many to try to "Put Yourself in His Place," even if it is only in a horse's place. The question is not, "Can they reason or can they speak?" but "Can they suffer?"

THE RICH POOR HORSE AND THE POOR RICH HORSE.
BY MRS. C. M. FAIRCHILD.

The poor rich horse, driven by a tall coachman with high hat and white gloves, looked very gay as he pranced up to the door of an elegant establishment on the avenue. The breast of the noble creature was covered with foam, and he held his head very high. His mouth was stretched wide open, and he tossed his head up and down and back and forth, and pawed the air with his fore feet. So high were his eyes—almost looking towards the sky—that he scarcely seemed able to see a fat old dray horse that stood near, regarding him with a sort of sleepy wonder, and considering him as belonging to another "set" than his, entirely. The old horse did not suppose it would do any good to pass the time of day with his neighbor, as the rich horse undoubtedly regarded himself as far too grand to communicate with such a humble personage, so he changed the bit around in his mouth, and was just about to drop into a gentle doze when a sound of distress from the rich horse caused his plain neighbor to open his eyes wide and to regard the former with considerable curiosity, which at length expressed itself in this wise: "You look very gay, neighbor; are you not comfortable with your fine silver-plated harness and shiny trappings?"

"I can hear you, though I can scarcely see you," answered the poor rich horse, "for my harness, although undoubtedly very handsome, is a perfect torture to me. You can see for yourself how my head is tied up by a new-fangled contrivance they call an over-check. My eyes are almost blinded by the glare of the sun, and my neck aches, and my head throbs, and I am really quite miserable."

"I don't know much about check-reins," bluntly said the rich poor horse, "and I have never hauled fine ladies around in their carriage. I supposed, by the way I have seen them petting you with their soft white hands, that they wouldn't want you to be dressed up so you would be uncomfortable or suffer by it."

"O, they don't think," sighed the poor rich horse, "they doubtless suppose I have a very fine time with nothing to do but draw this pretty doll's wagon. If I could only have my choice I would change places with you. I would rather haul a dirt-wagon without any check-rein on than to be dressed up in this fine style and suffer as I do."

"You'd find the dirt wagon pretty heavy hauling," replied the rich poor horse.

"But I'd have my neck free and be allowed to exert my full strength doing it," retorted the poor rich horse with some spirit, and as he gave an extra strain at his check-rein, the rich poor horse noticed the blood was starting from the corners of his mouth. "Is it the check-rein that makes your mouth bleed?" asked the rich poor horse.

"Oh yes! I'm getting quite used to that. Very often my mouth is so sore I can scarcely eat, and then they think I'm ill, and a surgeon with a great long name—v-e-r-y-t-y-r-a-n-n-y I believe they call him—comes in with a black bottle, and ties up my head, and pours some dreadful medicine down my throat, and whips me when I kick at him."

The rich poor horse now opened his eyes wide and surveyed his companion under the light of some new idea.

"Well, you have a nice stable to stay in, don't you? Now I have nothing but a plain barn and no padding. To be sure on cold nights I have straw up to my knees; but I don't have any blanket, and my hair gets rough and shaggy."

"Oh dear," sighed the poor rich horse, "I would much rather have your coat of fur, and wouldn't care how rough it is. If they would only let me have the hair that belongs to me it would be much more comfortable than a blanket. They cut off my hair and I feel every chilly wind that blows. I don't dance around as you see me doing because I feel gay and happy, but because I am perfectly miserable. Sometimes they make me wear the over-check and blinders, and then it seems as if I would lose my wits entirely. Little then can I see but the sky and the tops of people's heads; and if I stumble or run away, when I am afraid of something I can't see, the driver whips me where my hair has been clipped, and I can't say a word back."

"O, well, you don't have much hard work to do," said the rich poor horse, "you ought to appreciate that and make the best of your condition."

"I'll change places with you at any time," replied the poor rich horse. "My load becomes heavier than yours commonly is, because I am so tied back and curbed and reined, that half my strength is spent trying to relieve my aching muscles and neck. When I don't have to wear the over check, then they put on the bearing, (check-rein) rein, which is no better. And then when we fashionable horses grow old, and lose our style and spirit, we are sold to somebody who forgets we are not used to labor which develops the muscles, and we are whipped when we can't pull heavy loads, and have to endure exposure and all sorts of other hardships when the least prepared for them."

"Poor rich horse," said the compassionate attache of the dray, "I think I will try and be content with my lot after this."

Just then the drayman came around with some nubbins of corn. The gay coachman mounted his box and with a crack of his whip sent the poor rich horse flying down the street. The rich poor horse rubbed his nose on his master's shoulder and told him what he had heard about poor rich horses, and the two jogged off together the best friends in the world.

THE CURB BIT.

(Extract from essay of E. M. Collins in the "Bar Harbor Record.")

The curb bit is used even more than the check-rein, and many persons who are thoroughly convinced of the cruelty of the latter will use the curb without scruple.

This, in a way, can be made to take the place of the check, for if the strap or chain passing under the jaw is only tight enough the coveted quality of high-headedness can be obtained to nearly as distressing a degree as with the check.

But at what a cost to the poor animal! His jaw is all the while in the most cruel kind of a vise: the action of the saliva in his mouth is impeded, and a quantity of froth surrounds his mouth, which he flecks off in his nervousness. Now and then the froth is tinged with red—this is when the bit, pressing hard against the sides of the mouth, pinches the thin lining to the point of drawing blood; the tongue is compressed so that often times it is of a dark purple, or even black, and the underlip is quivering constantly, which alone tells of intense suffering. All these signs are visible whenever the curb bit is used with the strap or chain tightened. When the strap or chain is loose not so much pressure is felt, and the bit is little different from an ordinary plain one. In the majority of curbs used it is not the bit itself which causes so much suffering to the horse world, but the evil lies in the strap or chain which is fastened to the rims of the curb and tightened under the jaw.

The common plea for the use of the curb is that t is a safeguard against accident in case the horse becomes unruly. While in a very few instances the curb may perhaps have helped to control a fiery, vicious orse, by the intense pain caused, almost always it tends strongly to spoil a horse's disposition, irritating him and making him unwilling to obey. Many of the runaways are caused by the animals getting infuriated by the curb, and reaching the point where the pain is unbearable. Another plea for the curb is that the horses known as "pullers" can not be safely driven without it. The fact is that with many horses it only causes them to be more stubborn, and they get into the habit of bearing down on the bit and feeling its resistance, and expect the contest every time they are taken out. Horses are often broken of the pulling habit by being driven with a plain bit after having been used with the curb, and through kindness instead of brute strength, have become good drivers. The use of this bit destroys the delicate sensitiveness of the mouth, a quality which is so desirable in a good driving horse. * * * * * * Often owners leave the entire charge of their horses to coachmen and grooms, who are willing to resort to any methods whereby their turnouts may be ranked among the smartest, regardless of the suffering of the poor creatures in their care. These grooms are always strong advocates of the curb-bit.

TEACHING TRICKS.

CHAPTER XII.

Since there are so many people desirous of knowing how to drive a horse without bridle or lines, I have concluded to use a little space in describing this feature of the horse's education.

While I do not advocate it as being a universally practical way of driving a horse, yet it is possible to so thoroughly train the horse to the signals of the whip that he can be controlled more reliably under excitement and in case of danger than it would be possible to manage him with bridle and lines. This statement will no doubt sound erroneous to those who are not profound in the science of horsemanship; nevertheless it is true.

By having a horse trained in this way, it shows to the public to what extent it is possible to educate a horse when he is diligently and persistently dealt with

It would be unreasonable to expect any one to accomplish this feat who is not possessed of strong will power and self-control; especially to control a highly-bred spirited horse; and this is the only kind with which such education can be fully relied upon.

There are a number of different ways to teach a horse to drive without lines, but I shall not attempt to describe any except my original process.

DRIVING WITHOUT LINES.

My plan for teaching a horse to drive without bridle or lines, is first: Turn the horse loose in an enclosure about twenty-five feet square, take an ordinary buggy whip and go into the enclosure with him and overcome the fear of the whip and teach him to have implicit confidence in you, by the process that I have explained under Colt Training. After he has learned to come to you at the command "Come Here," and shows no fear of the whip while you gently wave it over his head and body, and will follow you all about in the ring, you then have a good foundation laid for further instruction. Put the horse away until the next day, when you should take him back to the same place and proceed to teach him the signals of the whip. Stand close to the horse's hip and take a short whip and tap lightly on the right shoulder, until the horse, in anticipation of driving a fly off, will swing his head around to where the tapping is; step forward quickly and hand him a few oats, or a small piece of apple, almost in the act of turning his head around. Step back and continue the tapping and rewarding. After a while, in his eagerness for the reward, he will take a step or two to the right when the tapping begins; then caress him and treat him very kindly for that act. By this process in a short time you will have conveyed your idea to the horse that when he is tapped on the right shoulder that means for him to turn in that direction. As soon as he barely understands what you want of him you should put him away for that time. At the next lesson you should give a repetition of the tapping on the same side until he will respond readily in that direction; after which commence tapping on the left side and reward as before. Both sides must be trained separately and thoroughly, then you may drill alternately. Now you may have an open bridle on him, with short lines to come back about as far as his tail; but only to be used when needed to restrain him, or to convey your idea to him. Your whip at this stage should not be over five feet long, and you should stand directly behind the horse. While you are not compelled to use the lines you should have hold of his tail with one hand. Allow the whip to extend directly over his body so the end of it will extend about to the middle of his mane, and the position of the point of whip you wish to familiarize him with, for a signal to go straight ahead, should be about two feet above point of shoulder. The signal you wish for him to stop for is, raising the whip and holding it in a perpendicular position. The action you may use to associate the meaning of this movement, and position, is: just as you raise the whip so the horse can see it, pull hard on the lines and say "Whoa!" all at the same time; and in a few repetitions he will stop when he sees the whip raise, knowing that means a "severe pull" if he doesn't stop. The first few times he stops without the pull, step forward and reward him. A great deal depends upon how you give the rewards.

If they are given in a manner so that the horse can fully comprehend it was complying with your wish, it will be a great help to you in fixing the impression upon his brain; but if it is not given in the right manner the reward will be worse than none at all. After he has the idea pretty well learned to stop when the whip is raised, you should raise the whip and give him a slight stroke around the neck and immediately raise the whip again. In a short time he will understand that when the whip goes up, that means punishment unless he stops quickly. In this way you reduce the power of the "pull with the lines" directly to the signal of raising the whip.

On the same principle you finally teach the signals of turning by giving him a pretty smart tap on the lower part of the shoulder and immediately place the point of the whip three or four feet in that direction. Should he attempt to jump and go ahead too much, you can hold him in check with the action and signal to stop him. You should now have a good whip about seven or seven and a half feet long. Right at this stage you will find that it will require skillful manipulation of the whip, so there will be no mistake made on the part of the trainer. You cannot have a horse reliably trained in this way, in excitement and under all circumstances, without some reserve power with the whip. After he has been driven for awhile, and obeys the foregoing signals well, you may then teach him to back at signals. The position of whip for this signal should point back over your shoulder at an angle of about forty-five degrees.

To convey your idea to the horse, you should put the lines on him; and when you move the whip backward and forward in that position, give the horse little quick jerks with the lines until he understands that the whip in that position means "back." Now to reduce the compulsory part of it to the whip stand on the near side well back toward the hip, so that the lash of the whip will reach over his head. Tap him over the head a few times in connection with the backward movement of the whip. Tap lightly at first, then a little harder, until he will step back freely, then caress him. Now if he should fail to respond to the signal when you have no bridle on him, you can force him to do so by tapping him over the forehead. When you want him to start or go faster touch him on top of neck or back. The signal for "steady," or to go slower, is to elevate the whip about half way up; as soon as he comes down to a walk, lower the whip again. The single foot strap will greatly assist in teaching the signals meaning Steady and Whoa.

When a horse is trained as just described, it makes him appear much more intelligent than he otherwise would, and he will attract attention wherever he is seen.

TO IMITATE A BALKY HORSE.

It seems foolish to instruct the public how to teach a horse to balk; for my observation has convinced me that they have a better knowledge of this particular feature than any other branch of horsemanship. However when a horse is educated, the trick of "acting the balky horse" is the most amusing trick that can be taught him. Yet the process of teaching it is exceedingly simple; probably this accounts for so many people having their horses trained in this way (unintentionally, however.) Have the horse hitched to a buggy with his head towards a building, or high fence, so that he will not be so eager to go ahead; now you may ask him to go, and when he attempts to start, set him back gently with the lines; keep it up until he shows some hesitancy about starting. After shaking the lines and slapping him on the hips, then immediately caress him. Allow your strokes of persuasion to be but little harder than caresses at first. If he is thoroughly acquainted with the right meaning of the command "Get up!" you had better use some other words at first, that will not be so likely to encourage him to start. Say, "Go on! Now! What's the matter with you?" etc., until he associates the balking with some of your balky actions; then you may use commands and slaps that under any other circumstances he would fully understand to mean something directly opposite. Do not try to teach this trick thoroughly, in one lesson, or you might have trouble in having him start off pleasantly when you are ready for him to go. This is one of the most interesting tricks my regular exhibition horse performs. He imitates the balker to perfection, without bridle or lines; will turn his head around to his side and utterly refuse to move although enough men are pushing on the buggy to almost slide him, and holloing "Get Up"! whipping him with stuffed clubs, etc., will not start him until the proper signal is given him to go.

TEACHING TO KICK AT COMMAND.

If your horse is an ill-dispositioned animal it would not be advisable to experiment much with this trick, for it would be easy to make that kind of a horse irritable and possibly cause him to kick without command.

A horse of a mild disposition may be taught to perform this act without any risk of spoiling him. Take a pin in right hand and prick the near hind leg with it and say "kick." When he makes a move with his foot backwards, reward him. Repeat the pricking and rewarding for a few minutes each day and he will soon learn to kick with the left foot when you say "kick." Or, if you would want him to kick at signal without word of command, you can teach the signal by having a small tack in your whip and proceed as before. In a few lessons he will kick as soon as you point the whip toward that leg.

TO LIE DOWN.

Secure a suitable place before you attempt to teach this trick, which should be a nice soft grassy spot, or have the ground covered with a good coat of straw. There will be no better way to have him understand what you want him to do than to put him down a few times by my process of laying a horse down, as described under Subjection. While he is down treat him with the greatest attention and kindness; give him some oats out of your hand, walk around him a few times, and then caress him again. Do not keep him lying very long at one time. After two or three lessons you will only need to stand on off side, reach under him, raise near front foot with your hand and draw his nose a little to you, and say "Lie Down," and he will obey your command. A few lessons more and you may only touch him on the knees with the end of your whip and he will go down. Don't fail to always use the same words: "Lie Down."

TO SIT UP.

After you have taught him to lie down, you may put an ordinary riding bridle on him, ask him to lie down, then get behind him, step on his tail while you hold the bridle reins in your hand, say "get up."

TELLING AGE.

Have a small tack placed in a whip close to the lash of it; prick him on the back part of the front leg. He will raise the foot and put it down with a thud, to get vengeance on the "fly." Have him do this two or three times, then reward him for it by caressing him. When he understands that when the whip is pointed toward the leg it means for him to paw, you may raise the whip quickly and let the end of it strike him under the chin, and he will soon learn to stop when you raise the whip. By taking the same position every time he will soon know what you want him to do by a movement of the finger, or a slight bending of the body. You may now ask him how old he is; and when he strikes the ground as many times as he is years old, you may change your position and he will have told you his age. Or you may substitute any question you like; for instance: How many days in a week are there? How many are three, six and eight? He can solve problems like this as well as tell his age.

TO MOUNT A PEDESTAL.

Have a strong platform made about four or five feet square, and about one foot high. Place one of the horse's feet on it and pinch the other leg a little and he will soon let his weight on the foot that is on the platform. Get him up several times with his front feet; then assist him in getting a hind foot up, and encourage him to come forward. When he is up with all four feet reward and treat him kindly as described for other tricks. It will only take a little more patience to have him get several steps higher by having everything arranged substantially, so that he will not get hurt in getting down. After he thoroughly understands what you want him to do he will go through the performance without prompting. I remember several years ago when I first began to study the subject; I had one of my father's colts trained to get on top of almost anything he could get his feet on. While he was being shod one day, the blacksmith placed his front foot on the little clinching post to clinch the nails of his shoe, when the colt put his whole weight on that foot and raised the other high up over the blacksmith's back as if hunting for a still higher place to put his feet. Fortunately there was no damage done except badly frightening the blacksmith.

HOW TO TEACH A HORSE TO TEETER.

After he has been taught to get on blocks, platforms, etc., it will be almost a continuation of that feature of training. Have two or three strong boards about sixteen feet long nailed together so the teetering board will be about thirty inches wide. Allow it to lay almost flat on the ground the first few times you lead your horse over it; then elevate by degrees. The fulcrum should be about six inches wide and just a few inches high until the horse learns to balance himself well. It will assist greatly to have the Excelsior Bridle on him. As he gets near the center of the board you can step back in front of him to the other end of the board; by having hold of the bridle you can keep his attention so that he will not jump off while you carefully teeter him. After he gets accustomed to the teetering motion, move him up to the middle of the board; then get on one side of him, and by the aid of the whip, with light taps, he can be made to move one of his feet backwards and forwards. You can elevate the fulcrum to about a foot and a half high. By having it any higher than this you would require a longer board. A few lessons and he will run up on the board at command and perform this most beautiful act.

TEACHING TO KISS.

Stand in front, a little to the left of your horse, and give him a small piece of apple with your left hand; then hold your hand closer to your face and allow him to take his reward. After a while you may have a piece of apple on a small stick, two or three inches long. Hold one end of it in your mouth and let him take it off the stick while the other end is in you mouth. Always use the word "kiss" when you want him to do the act. In a few lessons he will put his nose within a few inches of your face at the command "kiss me," without the reward. It would not be desirable to have the horse place his mouth against your mouth; therefore when he makes an effort to reach his nose toward your face, you must accept it as complying with your wish. This trick will be quite easy to teach.

TO TAKE HANDKERCHIEF OUT OF INSIDE COAT POCKET.

Lay a handkerchief in your hand and put a few oats on it. Allow the horse to eat the oats; he will naturally get hold of the handkerchief. After he gets eager for the oats you may raise your hand with handkerchief and oats, to your breast and slightly under your coat. Now that he has learned that you want him to take hold of the cloth, you may put it partly under your coat without the oats, and when he takes it out, you may give him some oats out of your hand. In a short time he will root his nose under your coat back under your arm to find it, in anticipation of his reward. Now that he understands what you want him to do a caress will do as well as a reward, and he will soon comply with your wish when you say "Find it."

TO CARRY AN ARTICLE IN THE MOUTH.

This trick will have been nearly taught if you have first taught him to take a handkerchief from your pocket. Take a cloth and mash a part of an apple in it and place it where the horse is accustomed to be the most and tell him to "Bring it." When he follows you around with it for a little distance, caress and talk encouragingly to him. If it is a basket you wish to teach him to carry, you may wrap the same cloth around the basket handle and he will finally learn to associate the command that you use for "bring" or carry, with the basket. I shall only give space enough for some of these simple tricks, so that even an amateur can know how to begin with them.

TO FIRE A PISTOL.

Secure the pistol firmly to a post or as high as the horse can conveniently reach; attach a string to the trigger and a small wisp of hay to the end of the string; have it arranged so that by pulling at the hay the trigger will snap. (Do not have the pistol loaded, or it will frighten your horse so you cannot get him near it again.) Take the horse up to this until the hay attracts his attention; he takes hold of the hay, the trigger snaps; he eats a bit of hay, and is satisfied; so are you. Repeat. When he does this readily put a small rag with but a very little hay, then when he pulls give him some oats and caress him. Leave out the hay altogether when he becomes accustomed to pulling the rag; the pistol can be capped. The explosion will startle him; then by kindness you must get him over this; then add a very small charge of powder, but not before he has become accustomed to the snapping of the caps.

TO TEACH TO STAND ERECT.

Put on the First Form War Bridle, as described under Subjection. Have him reined up a little. Take a buggy whip in right hand and cord in left, and say "Stand up!" or "Up!" at the same time give slight jerk with the cord and quickly move in front of him; if he makes the least effort to raise his front feet off the ground reward for it. If he does not show any inclination to get up, you may rein him rather tight until he will make an effort; then stop and caress him. You should not continue to drill him but a few minutes at a time, and not more than twice a day. Don't fail to use the words "Stand up," with every effort you make to have him stand up, so that he will associate the power of your simple devices with the command.

TEACHING TO JUMP.

Have a railing about a foot and a half high arranged on the ground where there is ample room for the horse to have a little run. After you have taught him to follow you on a run, you may run in front of him and jump over the railing first, and say "jump!" In most cases he will follow you; but if he should want to go around it, or avoid jumping, you should put on him the Pulley Breaking Bridle; the cord should be about fifteen feet long; a little admonishing with it will cause him to jump. As soon as he gets your idea that you want him to jump, you may remove the cord and teach him to jump at command. Having the outside end of railing against a building will greatly assist in keeping the horse in bounds. In teaching any trick always take him to the same place where you began teaching him. Never leave one trick until it is thoroughly understood; by leaving a trick half learned, he will always perform it as being half understood, and will spoil the effect of the performance.

TO SAY "YES."

Stand in front of him, a little to one side; prick him very lightly with a pin on the breast; thinking it is a fly he will put his head down to chase it off; reward him for so doing, and continue until the slightest indication of extending your hand toward his breast will cause him to lower his head. Always bear in mind that to teach him to do the act at command, it will be necessary always to associate the word that you want him to learn, with the act; for instance: If you want the horse to learn that the word "yes" means for him to bow his head, always speak that word when you prick him on the breast, and he will soon learn that "yes" means for him to make a bow. After proper rewarding for obedience, he will not only do the act through fear of punishment, but will do it because he knows he is well treated for complying with your wish.

TO SAY "NO."

Go to left side of horse near the shoulder, holding a pin in your right hand. Prick him lightly on the neck near the shoulder. He will shake his head; caress him and repeat the word "No," and the act, until he learns that "No" means for him to shake his head. This trick should not be taught for some time after teaching him to say "yes." By practicing them close together he will invariably run one into the other, and you will fail to teach either one correctly.

TO GALLOP.

Take the horse into an enclosure about thirty feet in diameter; turn him loose and start him quickly with the whip. When he gallops around the ring a few times, stop him and reward. Start him at the same place, use the same word ("Gallop") and have him go the same way around the ring every time. This will assist you greatly in conveying your idea to the horse. Do not teach any other trick of a similar character until this one is fully learned.

TO WALK.

Start your horse around the ring in the opposite direction from which you taught him to gallop. When he has gone around several times, stop him, and pet him. Should he go too fast use the word "Walk" and have him go slower by making a slight move to the front of him. Another way to teach the word walk, is while in ordinary driving or while the horse is trotting give him the command "Walk!" and immediately give him a raking pull with the lines sufficient to bring him to a walk. By repeating at short intervals, you will be pleased to know that your horse will have learned the meaning of "walk" in two or three lessons.

TO TEACH A HORSE TO TROT AT COMMAND.

This can be done while driving; while walking along say "Trot!" and give him a slight stroke with the whip. Be sure to give the command "Trot!" before you give the stroke. In a short time he learns that "trot" means to get out of a walk, or a stroke of the whip surely follows. With a little further training in the ring, he will start off on a run when you ask him to "Gallop," and on hearing the word "Trot," he obeys by slowing to that gait, and the command "Walk" brings to that gait.

TO TEACH A HORSE TO APPEAR VICIOUS.

In teaching this trick it would only be necessary to refer you to the many persons who have made their horses vicious, by their improper actions, in trying to train them for general use. About all that is required in teaching this trick, is to tease the horse a little and then pretend to be afraid of him, by running from him. After he has learned that he can make you run, he will lay his ears back and act vicious whenever you act timid; and when you stand your ground firmly, he will act as gentle as any horse. This makes one of the most sensational tricks that a horse can be educated to perform.

A FEW GENERAL HINTS ON TRICK TRAINING.

A young trainer must not fall into the mistaken notion that mere quickness in picking up a trick is the best quality in an animal. There may be such a thing as learning a lesson too rapidly, and what is learned with but slight effort is sometimes forgotten with equal readiness. Another thing, too much should not be expected of one pupil. Public exhibitors are able to show a large array of tricks because of the number of horses they have, each as a rule, knowing comparatively few of these tricks, or, in the case of some of the "sensational" tricks, perhaps only one. Still any animal of ordinary capacity ought, with proper tuition, to be able to learn a sufficient variety to satisfy any reasonable trainer. Judicious management on the part of the exhibitor will often make a variety of tricks out of a single one which the animal has been taught. The first essential for success in training animals is patience. At first in teaching some difficult trick many lessons may be given without the slightest apparent impression being made upon the mind of the pupil and an uncommon degree of patience and good temper is required to bear up against such discouraging results. By and by however, the pupil will suddenly appear to realize what is required of him, and will perform his task with surprising accuracy at the very moment his teacher is about to give up in despair. Then each successive lesson is learned with greater ease and rapidity than the preceeding one; the weariness and disappointment of the trainer is changed to pleasure at his success, and even the horse appears to appreciate his master's joy, and to take pride in his performance. As it is impossible to explain to an animal what is required of him he can be taught an action only by its constant repetition until he becomes familiar with it. When he knows what you want him to do he will in almost all cases comply with your wishes promptly and cheerfully. For this reason punishment should be avoided, unless the animal is wilful. As a general rule it interferes with the success of the lessons. **If the pupil is in** constant fear of blows, his attention will be diverted from the lesson; he will dread making any attempt to obey for fear of failure, and he will have a sneaking look which will detract materially from the appearance of his performance. This is the case with the horses instructed by a trainer in our locality who "trains his horses with a club," the animals never appearing as well as those taught by more gentle means. A sharp word or a slight tap with the whip will as effectually show your displeasure as the most severe blows. It is both cruel and unwise to inflict needless pain. It is well to make use of various little tidbits as rewards for successful performance of tricks. These serve as a powerful incentive to the animal as well as to show him when he has done right. Withholding the accustomed reward when he fails or but imperfectly performs his duty is much more effective than any corporal punishment. The repetition of the lesson until the animal will himself perform the required action, and the bestowal of these rewards whenever he obeys your order, is really the main secret of training. Of course there are many important details in the practical application, and many clever devices resorted to by trainers to increase the effectiveness of tricks, as well as skilful combinations of simple tricks to produce elaborate and astonishing feats.

PERSONAL EXPERIENCE.

CHAPTER XIII.

As I have often been asked what ever possessed me to engage in such a dangerous avocation as training colts and subduing vicious horses, I do not think it improper to give a few explanations why I am in this business, and also give a little of my experience in handling horses. I was born and brought up near Pleasant Hill, Ohio, on a farm, where I evinced somewhat of a talent for training colts, but never had the opportunity of developing this talent until at one time I was training one of my father's colts. As I think the circumstance connected with this colt is the identical one that started me in the horse training business, I will give you details of this case. The colt was about three years old, and I had driven him three or four times, when one Sunday afternoon I drove him to a neighbor's house. I had to cross a ditch and open a gate to get there, and when coming out I was obliged to leave the colt alone, about three rods from the gate, until I went back to shut it. I noticed the colt was a little excited and very doubtful about standing, but I thought I would start back, and if he made an attempt to start, I would grab the lines and set him back and show him that he must stand. He started and I grabbed the lines, but one slipped out of my hands, and it gave him too much of a side jerk, which excited and made him more restless than before. It had been my motto ever since I was a little boy, never to attempt to have a horse do anything without having him do it, so I tried him once more, expecting if he started again to manage some way to teach him that he would have to stand. But this time he got the start of me. I grabbed several times at the lines but "failed to make connections." He ran as fast as he could, upset the buggy, tore loose from it and ran home. I had already determined to show him that he would have to stand in that very place until I went back to shut the gate. When I got home I found the horse terribly excited; I then took the lines out of the rings and ran them through the shaft bearers of the harness, got behind him and intended to teach him that Whoa! meant to stand, but didn't more than get behind him than he started to run again. I knew of no appliance by which I could take the advantage of him except a crude form of War Bridle, which I made out of an old clothes line. About all the advantage it gave more than the lines, was that it made a slip loop around the lower jaw. With the aid of this clothes line, in about an hour and a half of hard work I succeeded in subduing him and making him perfectly submissive to stop and start at word of command, and also to stand until commanded to go. I then hitched him to another vehicle and drove him to the very spot that he ran away from, and made him stand until I went about three rods behind to shut the gate. One week after that I had him hitched away from home after night, when the hitching strap became untied; he turned around with the buggy, went home, and from all appearances walked every step of the way, and stood by the stable door waiting to be unhitched, just as if he had been driven there. The reason the colt did not run and tear the buggy to peices was because he thoroughly understood that the previous treatment was for running away. A few months after that time the colt was driven to a carriage, when the front wheel came off while he was trotting at a fast rate. The axle tree and weight of two persons came right against his heels so hard that it tore the skin and flesh off both of his heels, yet he was controlled and stopped in a very short time, with all this weight directly against his heels. This proved to me as well as to all who knew of this case, that his submissiveness under such excitement was entirely due to the treatment I gave him for running away. The idea struck me then that if it was possible to change a horse's character in so short a time, and so fix the impression on the brain that he would never forget his training, it would surely be something worth knowing, and I began handling horses and studying their nature from that time on.

 I had handled colts and bad horses for six months, and had fully made up my mind to control and educate horses, before I had ever heard of horse trainers or ever knew there was any body traveling in the business of "Horse Training," when one day, while calling on a friend, I happened to see a book on Horse Training. I immediately procured a copy of it, and studied the subject with renewed zeal. A few months later I saw a book advertised in a newspaper, which I sent for at once, and made inquiry and searched for other books that might be printed on the subject; but to my surprise these were the only books that I could find pertaining to Horse Training that were worth looking at. Neither did I have an opportunity of taking instructions under any Horseman, except at one public exhibition at Dayton, O. I went twenty-five miles to attend one of his evening exhibitions. With this slight exception I had to get all my knowledge through hard experience. Of course I got some very good theories from these books, but theory is not practice. Some of the first horses that I took to break were bad dispositioned colts and Texas ponies, (as I was just commencing to study and work in my new profession, I had to accept such horses as were brought to me for training,) and some of them were the very worst ponies in the country.

You will never know the narrow escapes, experiences and hardships that I went through with, in handling these ponies, unless you would go through with them yourself. At this time I had no books to get ideas from, nor any appliances by which to take advantage of a horse. I will have to admit I did a great deal of my work through main strength and awkwardness, yet I felt and saw that I was gaining ground, and learning new ideas and points every day. Not only did I have to work without an instructor, books or appliances, but I was laboring under all manner of disadvantages and opposition. The neighbors and people going along the road would make light of my work and say "I had better quit playing with colts and go to work." And my folks at home were terribly opposed to my handling horses, saying I would keep on until I would get killed, etc.

Father finally forbade me bringing any more bad horses on the place, saying that if I wanted to farm the place any longer he would not allow me to bring any more horses there to train. I told him that I had fully made up my mind, and resolved to make a horse trainer out of myself, if I didn't get killed in learning the business. When he saw the determination I had to master my profession, he submitted to my handling horses. At this time I had an irresistible desire, and almost an uncontrollable passion, for training colts and subduing vicious horses. I haven't farmed any since that time, but have had all the horses to train ever since that I could handle and a great many more. I have had from two to six colts and vicious horses under training all the time for nearly three years, and sometimes more, having all kinds of vices—kickers, balkers, shyers, halter pullers, runaways, and colts. After I had broken a few bad kicking horses known to nearly every body for their viciousness, and saw that they were made perfectly safe and gentle, they began to fall in one by one, and recognize my work. It was here where I originated my system of colt training. Some of the first colts that I had trained I gave two lessons a day, and turned them over to their owners in about two weeks. But I found that it was giving them too much in a short time; it brought their lessons too close together, and two weeks was not long enough to fix the impression on the brain. So I changed my plan of training to giving one lesson a day, and teaching them four weeks instead of two, making their lesson about one hour in length, according to my present system, as described in this book. I found that lessons given in this way would be remembered better than to give them two lessons a day, and there would not be so much danger of running the lessons into each other.

A very important point I observed, was to teach but one thing at a time. I learned through experience, that it was almost impossible to give the colt the first and second lesson both in one, or even in the same day. The first lesson is to teach the colt to keep its heels from us, its head towards us, and follow, while the next lesson we teach is to keep its heels towards us, its head from us, and go away from us; two ideas exactly opposite to each other. In trying to teach both ideas at one time it only confuses the colt, and the consequence will be to fail in teaching either point so that the colt will remember it. But I found by teaching the colt one command at a time, it would so fix the impression upon the brain that it would not forget it, and the next day I could teach it something directly opposite, and it would then retain both ideas. I soon learned that my system of colt training was not only the proper way of training colts, but that it was equally applicable to all spoiled horses; as it is almost invariably the rule for all spoiled horses, or any horses having vices, to have but little or no education at all. And how can you expect them to obey your command and act intelligently without first teaching them what to do? After you have subdued the bad, vicious, or unruly horse, and made him willing to do all that he understands, it is just as important and necessary to treat him with gentleness and kindness, and teach him what you want him to do, as it is to be gentle and patient with the colt. There is no better way of teaching them what to do than to follow my system of colt training. In all my private training of bad horses, the first thing I do is to give them a course of subjective treatment, to get them under control. Then I always give them a repetition of colt training. Controlling physical resistance is but a temporary bridge across a stream to enable us to build the real structure. So subjection is but the means for reaching the brain to remove the exciting cause of resistance. If the resistance is stimulated by fear, then show there is no cause for fear—if through real viciousness, then remove the sentiment by kind treatment—when the horse's reason can be moulded and instructed as desired. I claim there is no education in subjection any further than it teaches the horse we are his master.

It is simply getting a horse in shape or condition to be taught. If it is possible to gain a bad horse's better nature, and win his confidence through kindness, without any coercive treatment, which I think it is in a great many cases, it is the very best kind of subjection. But in nearly all cases where they are confirmed in the habit, it will be necessary to use coercive treatment to get them under subjection. I have tried to make every point so simple and plain that any one can easily understand there is no mystery in the control of horses beyond that of skilful treatment When managed according to the laws of their nature it becomes a very simple matter to subdue and control even the most vicious horses. Every horse made vicious or unmanageable, is so in reality through bad treatment. To be a good horseman you should always show by your actions and conduct, that you are a man, and that your real superiority over horses consists in the prudent exercise of your reasoning powers. A man must have patience and courage, if necessary, that borders on harshness, yet always holding himself within the limits of safety. Whatever the difficulties or failures, he should only exhibit the more care and patience, until successful. It is especially important that there be no foolhardiness, lack of judgment or carelessness, that will expose the horse to danger or accident. It is an invariable fault of those who claim any skill or experience in the management of horses to be over confident; to think too much of the little they know of applying the treatment, and too little of the difficulties and danger of resistance in the horse to be treated. A man who assumes to know all about horses, and can break any horse, etc., only gives to any sensible, observing man, the strongest proofs of his ignorance. The most ignorant men in the business are usually the greatest pretenders. Of course it will not be difficult for any ordinary man, by following my system of "Colt Training," to break the average bad colts and horses. But if the case is at all critical, success will depend upon making no mistakes and being thorough. Every failure is an undoubted proof of lack of judgment and good management.

In building a bridge, or any structure where large risks of life are involved, extraordinary precautions are taken to insure safety against accidents, by requiring much more power than is expected to be used at any time. Every part is tested as to its strength and weight far beyond what it is ever required to sustain, and when completed, is again proved, in order to give assurance of its safety. Now in the subjection of horses, especially those used for carrying and family driving, where lives are risked, they should be treated very thoroughly. I always give them such tests as they will never be likely to have in ordinary using and driving; for instance, driving kickers and runaway horses with tin pans and sleigh bells tied to the crupper of their harness, leaving them hang down and striking their heels every step they take. If they are nervous and excitable, I drive them over paper, under flags and umbrellas, rattle cow bells, tin pans, sleigh bells, beat drums, use horse fiddles, and make all the racket I can have stirred up about them. In this way give them to thoroughly understand that these objects and racket will not hurt them. After a few lessons of this kind the horse will take no notice of the usual minor causes of fear, such as a bit of paper flying up about him, an umbrella being carried in front of him, or the sudden playing of a band.

I learned through some of my hard lessons of experience that subduing a horse and making him docile in one place would give but little assurance of his being so at different places. He must have a repetition of subjective treatment at other places, especially the places where he had been in the habit of resisting, in order to break him reliably. We can subdue a horse in a building, then take him outside without giving him a repetition of the subjective treatment there, and he will appear almost as bad as he was before he had been subdued. We must take the advantage of him outside enough to show him we can control him outside the building as well as we can inside, although it will not require nearly as much work to make him gentle and submissive as it did in the building. We can almost subdue a vicious horse in the city amid all the busy noise and din, then take him into the country where everything is quiet, when he will become unmanageable there. But on the other hand, we can subdue a horse in the country, then take him to the city, and he will become unmanageble there. At one of the first places where I instructed a class I handled a very bad runaway mare; and after I had subdued her and made her submissive to drive without breeching, in the barn, I told them to throw the doors open, and I would drive her outside. They did so, and the **moment her head was out of the barn she sprang forth** like a deer, and ran across a ten acre field as fast as her legs would take her. I thought it very strange that she would take a spell of that kind after being subdued; but that was the way I learned it was necessary to give a horse a repetition of the treatment outside the building. As soon as I got the mare stopped, I took her out of the shafts and gave her a little subjective treatment, after which she drove as gentle on the road as in the building. After I had been handling horses for about a year, and had successfully broke all the horses brought to me, a great many of my friends advised me to go on the road as a "Horse Trainer," saying that I could make a great deal more money in that way; but knowing there were already too many professional men on the road that were not masters of their profession, I declined. I have always been of the opinion that if a man was not respected, and did not have a reputation at home, he could not make a success away from home. I also felt that I had a great deal to learn at home, and was determined to build a reputation as a horse trainer at home first. After I had handled a number of colts and horses in the immediate neighborhood and community, I advertised through the local papers that I would educate colts, and train kickers, runaways, balkers, shyers, halter pullers, etc. I

then received horses from adjoining counties, some coming as far as twenty-five and thirty miles. By handling horses in this way for a little over two years, I received a very good practical knowledge of different dispositions and vices in horses. In this way I learned to judge a horse's disposition at sight, almost as correctly as the man that owned the horse could describe it. The most serious objections I had to handling horses in this manner were: First—It was only the very worst dispositioned horses that were brought me to handle; and in the next place, they were owned by men that were timid, and afraid of gentle horses. Sometimes, after I would give them a course of training, and make them gentle and safe enough for any body to drive that knew enough to hold the lines, say "Get up!" and "Whoa!" they would use them a little while, and then let them know by their actions they were afraid of them. Of course the horse, after seeing he had opportunity, would frequently take it, and fall into his old tracks, when I would take him back and give him another course of handling, to get him under control again. I don't mean to say that all the horses that I broke were owned by timid or careless drivers, for I am glad to say that I handled horses for some of the very best horsemen in the country. I do not mean to speak disrespectfully of the men who are timid and afraid of horses, because we all know it is natural for some men to be afraid of horses of any kind. However, I am very grateful to all whose horses I have handled, and thank them very much fo their patronage; but as stated above, that was a very serious difficulty and objection to training horses privately. Any man that is a coward, afraid of timid horses, should have nothing to do with bad dispositioned horses, or any horse of doubtful character, for they will notice it and take advantage of it. Horses of that nature should be treated with firmness always; when you speak to them, speak with distinctness. When you want them to go, say "Get up!" in such a way that they will know that you mean for them to get out of their tracks immediately.

As I have omitted saying much about the whip, I will give you my opinion of it here. I am often asked whether I ever whip horses. I answer yes, but only when absolutely necessary. The only object in using a whip is to excite the fears of the horse, and make him respect your authority by slight punishment when he does a wrong action. It should never be used as an instrument of revenge, and no man is fit to break or educate a horse unless he can control his own temper. Fear and anger should never be felt by good horsemen. To a horse merely wild and timid, the whip should be but little used. Kindness will secure his confidence and remove his fears of you. A severe whipping may excite his passions to such an extent as to forever ruin him as a quiet driver. I never whip a horse unless I can do it in time, and in such a way that I am sure he will understand what the punishment is for. When we are not in a position that we can force submission, it would be far better not to touch the horse with the whip. When it is necessary to whip the horse, use a good bow top whip with a good cracker on it, and give him a sharp cut around the hind legs next the body, and speak sharply to him. Never give a stroke without accompanying it with the voice. Your voice and the crack of the whip effects as much as the stroke astonishes him. Don't whip too much. Just enough to disconcert and scare him. Never whip across the body; a few sharp cuts around the legs will frighten him that he will respect your authority. There are no horses so perfect that they should be driven without a whip in the buggy. It is true that there are a great many horses that require the use of the whip very seldom, but when it is needed, it is needed just as much as if it were in demand more frequently. For instance you are driving along the road, and your horse gets scared at a bit of paper or some other object, and he starts backwards, possibly towards a deep ditch. If you have no whip you have to let him go and take the consequences, if you have a whip you can give him a cut with it and save a collision. It is always safer to have a whip with you and have your horse understand what whips are made for. But do not abuse your power. I have known more flesh whipped off a horse in a day than you could feed on in a week.

After two years of this kind of experience of handling horses all the time, sometimes having as high as six bad horses at one time, I then felt that my experience and knowledge gained in this way might be worth something to the public; for I think people who use and handle horses need the instruction a great deal more than the horses do. I instructed my first classes in barns, but found that I could not accommodate all, neither could I handle horses so well on a cramped barn floor; so I purchased a large tent and set it up at the neighboring towns. I would generally solicit about a week for a class, and would have from one hundred to two hundred scholars in a class, charging one dollar and a half per scholar, giving them five or six lessons. I always gave them the privilege of having their money back on the last evening, if they were not satisfied with the instructions given them. I am happy to say that I have yet the first scholar to ask the rturn of his money. This gave me great encouragement, as also did the recommendations they gave me at nearly all the places I have had classes, which were not only unsolicited, but urged upon me. I offer some of the many received, substantiating my claims.

TESTIMONY OF OTHERS.

CHAPTER XIV.

The following is a local or sketch that contains my name the first time it was ever in print:

JESSE BEERY.

Prior to the days of Professor Rarey, horse taming was regarded as a humbug, but he demonstrated beyond a doubt that the most vicious horse could be subdued and rendered subservient to man through kindness. Since then quite a number have distinguished themselves as trainers of the noble animal. One of the most successful trainers in this part of the country at the present time, is the gentleman whose name heads this sketch. Mr. Beery is yet very young, but when a small boy he evinced a talent for training colts, and as soon as he was old enough to investigate the subject, he devoted his whole time to training horses. He takes any kind of a horse and trains it for its owner, charging only a reasonable fee for his services.

The next is an announcement of my first public exhibition, given about two miles from home, Sept. 1st, 1888. My admission fee was twenty-five cents, and there were nearly one hundred people present, including a few ladies:

Jesse Beery will give his first public exhibition Sept. 1, in Nate Iddings' large barn, near Pleasant Hill. He will show up his system of training colts and breaking vicious horses.

Prof. Jesse Beery, our skilled horse trainer, has at present in training six of the equines, which have natural and acquired cussedness. Among them is a fifteen year old kicker from Woodington, Ohio. He gives them "Jesse" every time.

A short time before my first exhibition, I purchased a very bad dispositioned colt, one that would balk, rear and plunge. I will describe her head, for I think it had about as many characteristics indicating a bad disposition as is generally found in one head. She had a very long head, narrow between the eyes and between the ears, had long ears, with plenty of long hair inside of them. Her eyes were small and set well back in her head. On account of her being so mean and ugly, I was determined to control her, and thought I would see how far I could teach her; before I quit I drove her by the signal of a whip, without bridle or lines. While driving her in a neighboring town (Covington) one day, the editor of the Gazette saw me driving her, and gave the following local:

Jesse Beery, of Pleasant Hill, gave an exhibition on our streets Monday, of the power of mind over a three year old colt. It was driven without lines or bridle, made to walk, trot, stop, or turn either way, all by the motion of the whip. It was a remarkable exhibition.

The following is from a class at Kessler Station:

One of the most pleasing and instructive exhibitions, held one mile north of Kessler Station, at Mr. G. W. Beck's barn, in the way of educating the horse, has just closed, with very gratifying success. Mr. Jesse Beery, of Pleasant Hill, Ohio, well and favorably known in this and adjoining counties as a trainer of vicious horses, and an educator of colts or young horses, spared no pains to teach the people how to train and educate the horse to make him man's most useful servant and true friend. He completely subdued and broke a kicking colt that the owner could not work. He thoroughly conquered an eighteen year old mare that had not been shod for years, so that she meekly submitted to be shod. We, as members of his class, can cheerfully recommend him as a master workman, and worthy of patronage in his profession:

A. R. Renner,	Benjamin Thuma,
Wm. Kerr,	Wm. Noonan,
Henry Jay,	Henry Blackmore,

J. B. Fagan,   Thomas Brown,
John Hale,   George W. Beck,

S. N. Pennel, New Waverly, Ind.

Prof. Beery will commence with a class in horse training, in Laura, O., on Monday, August 5th. Mr. Beery has won, and justly too, such a reputation among our people that it is only necessary to say to them that he is coming, and it insures him a hearing.

Prof. Beery, Pleasant Hill, closed his term of horse training at Laura, Saturday evening. He had a class of one hundred scholars. His large tent was crowded each evening. Mr. Beery is a success.

HOW TO BREAK VICIOUS HORSES.

Prof. Jesse Beery will instruct a class in Horsemanship in a large tent at Covington, on Thursday evening, November 7th, at 7:30. Please bring out your bad horses, as they will be handled for the class free of charge. There will be a number of all kinds of dispositions and characters of horses handled, viz: kickers, balkers, shyers, runaways, etc.

Later.—Having been members of Prof. Jesse Beery's class in horse training, at Covington, we heartily endorse his work, both as practical and reasonable, and recommend his lectures to all who would educate the horse to love and obey his master.

L. D. Falconer,
John Cassell,
Dr. H. D. Rinehart,
I. D. Hickman,
R. M. Shellebarger,
John E. Billingsby,
H. J. Perry,
C. B. Fletcher,
Samuel Hart,
Levi Falknor,
John Tobias,
Adam H. Jones,
A. E. Williams,
Abe Deeter,
H. Mohler,
James D. Rike.
N. N. Kreighbaum,
Asberry Basil,
Howard N. Brown,
W. C. Murray.
Sen. A. C. Cable,
Joshua Grubb,
Dr. John Harrison,
A. C. Deweese,
Henry Landis,
Jot Folckemer,
F. M. Perry,
C. M. Albaugh,
S. Mowery,
John Fox,
N. H. Tobias,
M. Koon,
S. B. Reiber,
J. W. Freshour,
Ira Mohler,
Henry Spitler,
Geo. Lindsay.
John F. Etter,
Ira W. Jones,
Perry C. Ratcliff,
R. M. Deeter,
Dr. A. S. Rosenberger.

The undersigned, at Troy, O., take pleasure in bearing testimony to the skill of Prof. Jesse Beery, of Pleasant Hill, O., in educating colts and training bad horses. We have seen the good of his work on green colts, halter pullers, kickers, shyers, horses bad to shoe, etc., and know that the impressions made are lasting. Any horse that has come through his system of training comes out obedient, gentle, and greatly enhanced in value.

Col. O. H. Binkley,	Geo. E. McKaig,
W. A. Eddy,	E. E. Moore,
Grant Myers,	Peter Brown,
Aaron Deeter,	W. J. Hall,
Mrs. H. A. Dye,	S. J. McCurdy,
Frank Sewell,	G. W. Graham,
C. D. Miller,	C. V. Hottel,
E. D. Hottel,	C. F. Miller,
C. L. Westhoven,	W. I. Tenny,
A. F. Broomhall,	John Landry.

At Phillipsburg I instructed the largest class that I ever had, some evenings having more than my tent would hold, and it has seating capacity for three hundred people. There were a number of men fifty and sixty years old in my class, who indorsed my system, but I will only mention the names of a few who are interested the most in horses.

We, the undersigned, have attended Prof. Jesse Beery's lecture on the education of colts and vicious horses, at Phillipsburg, O., and have been greatly instructed. His wonderful success proves that his system of training exceeds all others, and the practical illustration of the same receives our hearty endorsement. Mr. Beery deserves respect and esteem for his valuable instruction in the management of horses, and we wish

TESTIMONY. 193

to show our appreciation of his good work by heartily recommending his system to the public:

J. E. Barnes, I. N. Becker,
Wm. Detrick, J. R. Lees,
S. E. Folkereth, J. H. Falknour,
J. S. Becker, L. Pearson,
L. B. Harley, E. Pearson,
H. O. Landis. L. Harmon,
Ezra Folkereth, D. Heisey,
Casper Price, D. B. Crow,
C. C. Kossler, D. H. Warner,
Abe Emerick, David Isenbarger,
Albert Albaugh, M. D. S. Hutchison,
Samuel Heisey, Adam Minnick,
Harvey Klepinger, David Hess,
Adam Thomas, N. W. Rinehart,
Ellis Gray, Geo. Waybright,
Sam. Shelley, F. O. Thomas,
Elmer Shelleberger, E. W. Spitler,
Chas. Anderson, Harvey Hayworth,
A. E. Hickman, John Spitler, Sr.,
W. J. Pumphrey, J. C. Carns,
B. F. Spitler, Samuel Weaver,
C. E. Wagner, D. C. Falknor,
Isaiah Oaks, Theo. Falknor,
S. Binkley, Wm. F. Wagner,
Aaron Dohner.

The last class given before writing this book was

at Piqua, O., in the Ideal Rink, where I handled a number of extremely bad horses.—The following was in the "Dispatch:"

HORSE TRAINING EXHIBITION.—PROF. BEERY'S WONDERFUL HANDLING OF VICIOUS ANIMALS.

Prof. J. Beery, who is now instructing a class in the handling of horses of a vicious nature, is one of the most remarkable horsemen that it has been our lot to see. D. H. Heater, Esq., the popular Main Street grocer, is enthusiastic in his praise of Prof. Beery, and says that in all his experience he has never seen his equal, and that he has witnessed performances given by others, and between them there is no comparison. Mr. Heater is a horseman himself, and knows whereof he speaks. Last night Prof. Beery handled Prof. Wm. McMaken's two year old colt, John Daber's three year old, the kicking, biting and striking pony owned by James Hilliard, an animal noted for its viciousness, besides the "Warwick horse," an animal that would run at the drop of a hat. Every one of these were subdued and made almost as gentle as lambs. Nobody should fail to see this wonderful performance.

From the Editors of the "Dispatch."
WONDERFUL HORSE TRAINING.

A wonderful exhibition of horse training is now in progress at the Ideal Rink, given by Prof. Beery. Last night this gentleman subdued the vicious Hilliard pony, which had to be led into the rink by a rope about twenty-five feet long. In about three quarters of an hour the Professor had the animal under complete control, and it was gentle as a lamb. He has a number of other horses of a vicious nature that he will subdue. This morning he exhibited in front of the Dispatch office a three year old, driven to a buggy without the use of lines, and so completely was it under control, that it could be driven any where by signs of the whip. He is a wonderful horseman.

The previous extracts, notices, and recommendations, together with a number of others, have all been obtained within a radius of twenty miles from where I was born and raised. I always made it a point to satisfy every man whose horse I trained. Some of the first horses that I broke I made no charge for at all, although the owners wanted to pay me for my work. I took their horses partially to experiment upon, and gained enough knowledge pertaining to the art to repay me for my work. Often times men, through carelessness, would let their horses get the advantage of them and fall into their old habits, when I would take them back and make them gentle again without charge. However, I am glad to say that they were very few that it was necessary for me to take back. My patrons commenced talking for me, which was the best kind of advertising, and in this way I soon had more horses to educate than I could handle. I think I would be justified in saying that when I quit training horses at home I could have had at command five times as many colts and horses as would have been possible for any one man to handle.

I will say right here that I am indeed grateful to my neighbors and many friends, who, after looking at my theory and system of training from a rational stand point, gave me great encouragement in my efforts. It seemed that the very parties that "hooted," and made light of my work at first, after being in one of my classes, changed their views, and did a great deal more good in my behalf than parties who never opposed me.

I am often asked whether I teach horses to perform tricks. As training a horse to perform tricks is not very practical to the horse owner generally, I have never practiced teaching them in this way much. Of course, when a young man owns a nice little horse, and has taught him a few tricks, such as following, shaking hands, lying down, etc., it makes him appear more tractable and intelligent than he otherwise would. When I parted with the ugly colt that I had trained to drive without lines, I purchased a well bred two year old Hambletonian colt, which was exceedingly spirited, but didn't have a great deal more brain than the other colt. However, I made up my mind to drive him without lines. After teaching him the signals of the whip for a couple of weeks, I hitched him up for the first time he was ever driven. I drove him by the motion of the whip, without the use of lines, and have been driving him that way ever since. It being the first colt that I had ever heard of being driven in this way, without having first been driven with lines, I thought it quite

CHARLEY AS HE WAS ALWAYS DRIVEN.

a feat, especially on account of his having so much natural fear of almost every conceivable object. I controlled him with the motion of the whip, when it would have been almost impossible for any one to manage him with the lines in the ordinary way. Sometimes he would get so frightened that he would tremble, yet he would obey the signal of the whip, and march right up and feel of the object with his nose. I have driven him some of the darkest nights without bridle or lines, controlling him by commands. He knew right from left. When I would want him to turn, I would give the command right or left. He would turn as quickly at the word of command as by a signal of the whip. Now, if it is possible to teach and educate a horse to such a point, why cannot you teach them to obey the few commands necessary for their general use, and prevent or overcome the many vices which they are liable to fall into when carelessly managed.

 I wish to call your attention to the Vaughn mare, of Richmond, Ind. She was a high bred trotting mare, and her habit was to rear and throw herself, if not allowed to start as soon as put in shafts, or if held back, would refuse to go at all. On account of her remarkable self-will and treachery I will give a brief description of her. When she was hitched up it required four men to hold her, but she finally became so bad that she could not be hitched up at all. I gave her one lesson before the class, and (by getting privilege from the authorities of the city) I gave her one lesson on the street in the presence of hundreds of people. The police guarded the street, and we had full sway for about an hour, when she submitted to stay on all four feet, stop, start, and turn either way at command. Mr. Vaughn requested me to keep her in charge until I was sure she would be thoroughly educated, which I did. As I wanted to spend a short time at home I took her with me, and returned her in ten days a model driving horse. This was a valuable beast that was not worth anything when I took her in charge. I saw the owner a few months after I had handled his mare, and he told me that she had not made a bad move since I handled her.

The following experience, extracts and endorsements, have been received since my first books were published:

Richmond Daily Item, April 11, 1892.
WON THEIR CONFIDENCE.

Prof. Beery, by his excellent work here, won the entire confidence of all with whom he was brought in contact, and by his unquestionable correct methods must have done good here. He not only understands his business, but has a faculty of imparting it to others in a way that they not only can not help but understand it, but be impressed with it. In this he must do a good deal of good in improving the condition of the horse, not only in its better education but in its treatment. He treats the horse more as a child than as an animal, and the results he gets, even with horses that have been abused by never being taught anything, are wonderful, as well as gratifying.

A proof of this is seen in the case of the John Vaughn mare. She is a remarkably fine trotter but had been spoiled in the breaking and handling so that she had formed dangerous habits which hurt her value a great deal. Mr. Vaughn spent fifty dollars in money trying to have her taught by other trainers and got no benefit. In two lessons Mr. Beery had succeeded so well that Mr. Vaughn has sent the horse to Mr. Beery's training barn, at Pleasant Hill, where he will train her until he is satisfied with her.

Richmond Daily News.

The exhibition of Prof. Beery, which he calls a school, is attracting a good deal of attention and also doing a great deal of good here by educating the members of the class up to the handling of horses by rational treatment. It is so wonderful what he does with the most vicious horses, simply by following a few rules founded on common sense, that it seems as if anybody ought to be able to do it. He has a few rules, which seem to be, when simplified into the least possible compass:

Let your horse know what you want him to do so that he fully understands.

Let him know that he will receive kind treatment if he does it and will be corrected if he does not.

When you start out to make him do anything, make him do it thoroughly before you quit.

As the result of this treatment with the few appliances he uses he produces most remarkable results. One of them was in the Linn Mather pony. It had become so confirmed a halter puller that it had not been tied up either on the street or in the stable, for four years; it broke every halter. After fifteen minutes treatment last night he tied the pony to a post with a string and fired a pistol at its head and it hardly winked. A mustang which has been owned here for years, and was so smart a kicker that it would almost shave a man who came around its heels, was so completely subdued in fifteen minutes that he couldn't get it to kick. These and many other examples show the efficacy of his treatment.

A GOOD SYSTEM.

To whom it may concern:—Having attended the lectures delivered by Prof. Beery in this city on colt training and the management of vicious horses, I take pleasure in recommending him to all who may be in any way interested in the management of horses. By his system the intelligence of the horse is appealed to—this is particularly noticeable in his treatment of colts, which it is a real pleasure to witness. He is also equally successful in the management of vicious horses, which he controls with his safety appliances without any brutal treatment of the horse, first giving him to understand that he is master and then educating him. The ladies of this city have also been much interested and entertained by attending the lectures.

CHAS. N. HOWARD,
Mayor of Xenia, O.

TESTIMONY.

SKILLFUL HORSEMANSHIP.

West Liberty, Logan, Co., O.

March 14, 1891.

We, the undersigned, citizens of Logan and Champaign counties, take great pleasure in certifying that Prof. Jesse Beery's practical system of colt training and subduing wild and vicious horses was the greatest success ever witnessed in this part of the country. We further say that Prof. Beery is a thorough master of his profession, and we recommend him to the public in general.

F. N. Speece,
David Stayrook,
Wm. Thomas,
C. S. Shoulton,
C. P. Wallace,
G. Shoemaker,
S. P. Wolf,
H. M. Black,
John Kelly,
Josiah Kelly,
J. A. King,
H. N. Kiser,
John B. King,
L. Elliott,
Jas. L. Fink,
David Gill,
J. H. Gibble,
David K. Hooley,

L. E. Baldwin,
Couchman & Muzzy,
A. H. Couchman,
B. M. Cook,
H. A. Crockett,
J. H. Couchman,
Jeff Davis,
J. C. King,
D. G. King,
Fremont Kirkwood,
Jacob King,
D. G. Lakin,
C. C. Moffit,
J. Merritt,
J. G. Hunter,
S. Hanna,
A. H. Henkle,
Frank Hayes,

R. Hedington,
B. E. Harris,
H. Jones,
H. Mohr,
A. G. Miller,
Z. Nickerson,
O. M. Newell,
H. H. Newell,
N. C. Newell,
A. M. Yoder,
Rudy Yoder,

David Harr,
B. P. Hanum,
Jacob Platt,
J. M. Pitman,
John Pine,
James Randal,
J. C. Rock,
D. D. Smucker,
Wm. Stewart,
John Shragle,

EQUINE TRAINING SCHOOL.

Sidney, Ohio, Oct. 7, 1891.

An exhibition of subduing vicious horses, and training those unbroken, was given here on Tuesday evening, by Prof. Jesse Beery, who may rightfully be said to be a master in the work. It was the first of a series of lessons that will be given before classes interested in horses. His work was witnessed by nearly one hundred persons, to whom it was an interesting lecture, with practical demonstrations. The first subject was an unbroken colt, the property of Louis Kah, Jr. It had never had anything on except a halter, and was as green as a colt could be, with considerably more fire than the ordinary equine infant, being highly bred. The second horse was the meanest one, probably, in Shelby county. It was a four year old mare of A. C. Fry. The animal some time ago ran away with a load of furniture, and with divers other loads since. She frightened at paper, flags and umbrellas, and has always been unsafe for the best drivers. The Professor said the first thing she needed was to understand she had a master, and he would therefore throw her down a few times, to open a train of thought for her. He had hard work to do it, and when down he brought a string of tin pans and rattled them. She struggled in her fright and got up, but was thrown again and again, and each time the pans were tried. In five minutes she would not look at them, and loose paper was tried. This was too much, and for a time she would not give it a friendly sniff, but in the end concluded it was harmless. Hoisted umbrellas and waving flags were tried, and then she was permitted to rise and try all of them. She flinched at first, but at last she went around the ring with loose paper in her straps, flags in her bridle and an umbrella over her head. She did this without being held by the lines, and when the audience cheered she pricked up her ears and nodded her head as if in appreciation of the compliment. It was conceded that the handsome animal was worth a great deal more money when she went out than when she came in. Several ministers and a number of ladies were interested spectators. It was a practical lecture of great value, and the series to follow will do every one who sees and hears them great good.

The following is a recommendation written by one of the most prominent and highly esteemed citizens of

Urbana, where I instructed a class of about seventy-five scholars:

Mayor's Office.
Urbana, O., September 18, 1891.

This is to certify that I have attended the lectures of Prof. Beery, and can cheerfully recommend him to the public. I believe his system of training and handling young horses the best I have ever seen. His system for breaking halter pullers is unequaled. I was present when he handled some of our worst kickers, halter pullers, shyers, horses difficult to shoe, afraid of different objects, and that have various bad habits. It would be well for every horseman, blacksmith, or any one interested in horses, to attend his lectures and secure one of his books. I will personally guarantee satisfaction, and I hope that every one may see the Professor's wonderful power over horses, as well as his kind and sensible manner of breaking young horses and subduing vicious ones.

C. H. GANSON, Mayor.

Springfield Sunday News.

HORSE SENSE.

A Thing Which Should Always Be, but Which Rarely Is. Possessed by Owners and Drivers of Horses—Not One Horse in One Hundred is at all Properly Trained—The Training School and Tent Exhibits of Prof. Jesse Beery in This City Last Week—It

Will Be Continued This Week, With Exhibits on Tuesday and Wednesday Evenings.

The average man is generally well satisfied with himself and his knowledge of men and affairs, until he runs up against some one who is a specialist, who has mastered some branch of usefulness, and then the "average man" is dazed by his own ignorance.

Every community has a generous quota of self-made horsemen, who can tell you all the *modi operandi* of breaking and training horses. But when you bring them into the presence of such a master of horsemanship as Prof. Jesse Beery, who instructed a class and gave tent exhibitions in this city last week—then your self-made horsemen admit that they have to unlearn and "learn over again" the correct, natural and humane method of educating a horse.

It is a matter of daily demonstration that the average man and woman is either incapable of or will not devote the time and patience to properly educating their own children. It does not require then a very powerful mental effort to conceive how utterly faulty and bad must be the education bestowed upon "only a horse" by the aforesaid average man or woman.

Prof. Jesse Beery is a native and resident of Miami county, and his post office address is Pleasant Hill. He was born and raised on a farm, and is thoroughly established in the business, having been a professional trainer and educator for ten years, and has been giving public instruction and education in horsemanship for the past eight years. There is nothing mysterious nor occult, nor anything cruel in the Professor's educational methods. His tools or appliances consist wholly of straps or ropes, which are so adjusted as to give, when needed, complete control and mastery over the horse, and yet not injure him. Prof. Beery is noticeably kind and considerate in his treatment of all the horses placed in his care. He states that to subdue or "break" a refractory or vicious horse, young or old, is simply to educate it. The first step is to allay its fears, to teach it that you mean it no harm, and then to convince it that you are master, and that correction, not brutal or passionate, will quickly follow disobedience or willfulness.

The Professor has published a handsomely printed and bound book, illustrated from life, giving full and explicit instructions in the application of his educational system in horsemanship. The book has had quite a large sale in this city, and practical horsemen say it is the very simplest and best work of its kind they ever met with. Its system is natural and practical, such as appeals to reason and judgment, and is sure of producing satisfactory and permanent results in teaching a horse correct habits. The system is purely and wholly educational—the application of kindness, patience and firmness in training a horse i "the way he should go."

Tuesday evening he began with the Pullman kicking pony, which has an ugly record as a kicker. In a remarkably short period of time, by treating the pony kindly, and convincing it that when it kicked it only hurt itself, through the adjustment of the anti-kicking strap, the Professor had broken the pony of its propensity to kick, and had made a docile, tractable animal of it.

He gave a breaking-in lesson with the Kirkham sorrel colt, and in five minutes taught this utterly green pony to follow him about, without any kind of bridle, halter or harness. The Professor keeps reiterating to his pupils that the horse's nose is his fingers, and that to allay his fears or suspicions of any article, let him rub his nose against it. Also to caress a horse by patting him on the shoulder, not by stroking his nose; and that the trainer, or educator, should be easy and gentle in his movements about the horse's head, so as not to arouse his fears and resistance.

Wednesday evening the Professor gave the Kirkham colt a second lesson, teaching him the true meaning of "whoa," the most abused and misused word applied to horses. "Whoa!" or "ho," means to stop forward motion, to come to a stand-still when in action, and should never be used for any other purpose.

Thursday evening the Pullman kicker was given its second lesson and was driven around the tent, hitched to a sulky, with tin cans tied to his tail.

Dr. J. C. Oldham's mare, which shies at pieces of paper and other objects on the streets, and which is mortally afraid of electric street cars, was given a valuable lesson. She was finally covered with papers thrown all over her, and flaunted in her face, without frightening her in the least. Next day the Professor and Dr. Oldham gave her a lesson in regard to electric street cars, and taught her that they would not harm her.

Thursday evening the Kirkham colt was given a third lesson, and was as docile and gentle in harness as any old, staid, family horse.

Joe O'Brien's famous white halter puller was given a lesson that gave excellent results. This "critter" is full of other tricks and vices, but the Professor educated her to better sense and better habits.

The star of the evening was the Hanford Mexican roan pony, a regular beauty, but perfectly valueless by reason of incurable balking. All the local horsemen and equine experts have exhausted all expedients to cure the pony of this vice without attaining any degree of success. After two hours hard work Prof. Beery drove it around the ring repeatedly, but he confessed it was the toughest subject in his experience.

Michael Stoll's horse shied and scared at umbrellas and baby buggies, but the Professor cured it of this vice in one lesson. You could decorate him with umbrellas, open and shut a dozen of them in front of him, and wheel baby buggies all over him, without the least bit of a shy or scare.

The Hanford roan pony was given his second lesson, and was hitched and driven with perfect ease, showing no signs of balking. All the horsemen in Springfield say that this cure by the Professor is a masterpiece, and is one of the greatest achievements in horsemanship ever displayed in this city.

The Professor then gave an exhibit with his own trained and educated horse, driving it without bridle or reins, and giving no command save with a motion of the whip—not touching or speaking to the horse. The horse promptly and gracefully obeyed every sort of command.

F. P. Whitehead, the livery-man, undertook to drive the Professor's horse, but commands, yells, slaps, pulling and pushing couldn't start him. Mr. Whitehead retired from the ring amid roars of laughter.

So successful and satisfactory were Prof. Beery's instructions last week, that the class has prevailed upon him to return this week and give two more public lessons, or exhibits, Tuesday and Wednesday evenings, August 11th and 12th. A noticeable and pleasant feature of these exhibits is the large and animated attendance of the ladies. The Professor is a gentleman in his speech and actions, and possesses an enjoyable vein of wit and humor in his class instructions. His exhibits this week will be attended by crowds.

Daily News, Hamilton, Ohio.

WONDERFUL EXHIBITION OF HORSE TAMING.

Prof. Jesse Beery, the horse trainer, gave a very fine exhibition of the superiority of intellect and common sense over brute instinct and intelligence last night. The first horse brought in, was a wild young colt belonging to Adam Rentschler, which had never had a bridle or bit in its mouth. In a very short time the Professor had it under perfect control, bridled and bitted, and docile as a lamb. He next turned his attention to a halter puller of Everson's, which he broke in completely. His handling of Billy Schwab's shyer and Billy Schramm's runaway was remarkable. When he got through with these horses, waving flags, hoisted umbrellas, jingling sleigh bells, flying newspapers, the crack and smoke of pistols, were alike powerless to arouse in the animals more than a mild and good natured courageous curiosity. The Professor's only devices are a few straps, pads and the reins, employed at first to govern the horse.

Daily Times, Muncie, Ind.
WELL TRAINED.

Prof. Jesse Beery, the horse trainer, has one of the best trained pieces of horse flesh that has been shown in this city for some time. The horse is a bay, of medium size, and is driven by the Professor without lines.

Marion Chronicle, August 2, 1892.
BEERY'S HORSE SHOW.—MORE WAYS THAN ONE OF SUBDUING OUR EQUINE FRIENDS.

An entertainment that is at once instructive and

amusing, is given nightly at the tent of Prof. Beery, the horse trainer, on West Second street. Last evening the enclosure was well filled by the crowd of horse lovers, including a number of ladies and children, who were especially well pleased with the exhibition. Prof. Beery began his work at 8 p. m., giving a three year old colt its second lesson. The animal is a thorough bred, owned by Simon Koontz, and is possessed of great spirit and intelligence. Last evening he was taught to mind the bit, to heed the commands, Get up, and Whoa, was made to have perfect confidence in his master, and passed out of the ring a fairly well trained animal as far as he had been taken. The Professor's method of procedure appeals at once to the intelligence of the animal. He is given a command, and this command is immediately followed by one or two actions which convey instantly the idea of what is expected. An ordinarily intelligent horse, taken at the beginning and trained patiently by this system, will form in his youth habits of obedience which will stay with him, as he will on the other hand, acquire vicious habits, through careless or misdirected training. Trainer Beery makes the lesson interesting and his methods plain in talks as he proceeds with the training school. and the scholars feel themselves amply repaid by the timely hints and suggestions given in the course of the evening. After the colt had been put through his course, and had demonstrated the almost human reasoning powers possessed by the horse when approached in a common sense manner, the Professor announced as the next subject a bucking broncho, just taken from a herd of Texas ponies which are in pasture near our city. The animal, a small and well formed bay, was brought in and very cautiously handled by the assistants while putting the harness and safety ropes in position, as he had a reputation as a kicker, and had, but a few days since, seriously injured his owner. The pony showed his vicious qualities at the outset by throwing himself on his head and prancing over the ring on his hind feet. He seemed surprised when he failed to light upon his feet, which were jerked from under him in a summary manner, and he finally realized that he had a hard fight coming, and buckled to it with regular western pony stubbornness and grit. The way he kicked and bucked, would have put to shame a small earthquake, and he seemed to snort fire as he met with each successive defeat. The sport of the evening came when a number of clattering tin pans were fastened to his tail, and the air was full of sawdust and horse shoes for a few minutes, until he was finally subdued. The work began to tell on him, and he finally gave up the fight, after showing all the viciousness of which he is master. Mr. Beery showed conclusively in his handling of this animal last evening, that the Texan is no worse than the ordinary native bred horse, and that his early training leads to the wrong ends. He succeeded in preparing this kicker for a new beginning. The pony is now where the youngest colt would be before the confidence lesson is given, and will be treated as a beginner. After this "broncho eruption" had been subdued in part, the trained horse, Charlie, was shown to the audience, driven by signals of the whip, and put through his paces. The audience was dismissed with a promise of something new and exciting to-night.

Reporter, Logansport, Ind.
WITHOUT BRIDLE OR LINES.

Prof. Beery drove up on the side walk in front of the Reporter office last evening and invited the editor to take a ride behind his trained horse Charley. The horse had no bridle and the driver had no lines, but the writer having witnessed the Professor's skill, concluded that the ride would be safer than behind many a well harnessed steed. So away the unbridled horse sped, guided only by the whip in the driver's hand. Suddenly on Fourth street the Professor kindly warned the editor to hold his hat on. Then he held the whip horizontal, gave a yell, and then just touched Charley with it and away he flew. Riding behind a horse without a bridle going at 1:44, is about as sensational as going through a shackly railroad bridge on a lightning express running seventy-five miles an hour. When the Professor held up the whip, Charley put down his four good strong hoofs and slid about five feet, stopping quicker than any horse could be pulled down by reins. And he only stopped because he was trained to. There was no compulsion about the matter.

A THRILLING EXHIBITION GIVEN BY PROF. JESSE BEERY, THE HORSE TRAINER.

The tent of Prof. Jesse Beery, the noted horse educator, at the corner of Market and Second streets, was crowded last night to witness the performance. It proved to be the most thrilling of any entertainment given here in a long time and kept the audience in breathless suspense. All of his work was highly satisfactory and elicited the heartiest commendation. He dealt with an old and vicious kicker, an unreliable and treacherous high-bred two year old, and broke a colt, all with unvarying success and in an incredibly short time. Yesterday afternoon he cured a horse belonging to Dr. J. B. Shultz It had a bad habit of scaringat the cars. To-night he will manage one of the Logan Brewing Co.'s horses that is hard to collar; James Foley's horse that is afraid of paper; David Eckhard's kicker, and Hartell's colt.

The following is from a worker in the Humane Society, Lafayette, Ind:

HUMANE TAMING AND TRAINING OF HORSES.

Editor Courier:—May I be indulged with a small space in your widely read paper, to reach the many persons who sadly need enlightenment on the proper handling of that most valuable and intelligent animal, the horse, that I may appeal to them to take advantage of the opportunity now offered by the gentleman of undoubted accomplishments in horse taming and training, that is just now giving a series of lessons and entertainments combined, on the Y. M. C. A. grounds in our city.

His performances are truly wonderful, and all the while most gratifying to advocates of the humane societies, and all lovers of mercy and wise management in handling animals. It was highly gratifying to the writer to hear the gentleman say that if an animal proved intractable to all humane treatment, and nothing short of abuse would subdue him, he would advise the owner to humanely dispatch him. It was a significant fact that no over head check rein was used in any of the various contrivances and ingenious trappings applied in the handling of perfectly untutored and untamed colts. The entire principle evinces a superior understanding of the horse character; leading scoffers as to a horse's intelligence into a higher field of knowledge, and making them realize how unappreciative they have hitherto been of one of God's greatest creations, greatest blessings to man. When I recall some of the speeches which have been addressed to me during the years in which I have made some effort to intercede in behalf of mismanaged dumb brutes I realize fully the great need of the dissemination of just such knowledge as Prof. Beery is endeavoring to instil into the minds of his hearers. It may sound strange, my lady friends, but I do not think there was a person in this gentleman's audience more interested, more absorbed in his talk and performance than myself, of which I am sincerely proud. The horse and his capabilities are worthy of the time and attention of the best minds and high souls, and no dullard is ever going to develop all that is in him. Go to these performances and become enlightened on an important subject.

EVELYN McCORMICK,
Lafayette, Ind.

Morning Journal.

PROF. BEERY'S SUPERB HORSEMANSHIP.

Prof. Beery's training tent in the rear of the Y. M. C. A. building, was crowded to its capacity again last night. There were several very satisfactory experiments and the onlookers were highly entertained. The concluding exhibition was the subjugation of a vicious mustang belonging to the Citizen's natural gas company, and the result fully justifies his claim to subdue the most vicious animal without resorting to severe punishment. For this evening he will have a number of interesting "subjects," including the famous colt belonging to Mr. James M. Reynolds, an animal that defied all attempts at pacification until he was placed in charge of this trainer. The exhibitions are interesting and will well repay attendance.

Evening Call.
PROF. BEERY'S WORK.

Professor Beery gave an excellent exhibition of his power as a horse trainer last evening, and the tent could not hold any more interested spectators, a number of ladies watching the performance with mingled feelings of fear and pleasure. A shying horse belonging to Rev. P. J. Roche was broken of the habit so thoroughly that he can now be driven without any trouble. Before the lesson he shied at nearly every strange object. A pony belonging to Sam Murdock that had developed a penchant for heroic kicking received a lesson, and marched around the tent with a string of tin cans attached to his tail without lifting a hoof. He can now be driven with perfect safety to the vehicle. A halter puller was given a lesson and has reformed. A colt was given the third and final lesson and is now completely educated and ready to enter a useful career. The exhibition was wonderful in many ways and was well worth seeing.

Crawfordsville News.
ALL KINDS OF HORSES SUBMIT TO THE WILL OF PROF. BEERY.

The tent in which Prof. Beery gave his exhibition was comfortably filled last night. The audience had come to witness the subjugation of several of the meanest kind of horses, and in this they were not disappointed. A halter puller of the worst kind was taught a lesson that he will not soon forget. After the test the horse would stand up to the post like any sensible horse. A kicker lost his fondness for kicking. In fact Prof. Beery showed to the satisfaction of all present that he was a horseman of no little ability, and that horses with any degree of meanness could be conquered by him. To-night he will handle the meanest mustang pony in the town. A standing reward of five dollars is offered to any man who will go in a box stall with him. Besides these there will be several other horses taken through a course of sensible training.

While at Lafayette, Ind., I ran across one of the most vicious brutes that I ever came in contact with. It was a finely built five year old gelding, belonging to Mr. Jas. M. Reynolds, a wealthy citizen of Lafayette.

Before closing my exhibition the first night I announced that if anybody had any vicious horses they could bring them the next evening. Mr. Reynolds stated that he had a vicious colt that he would like for me to subdue, but the colt was on his farm six miles from town, and that no one could approach him on account of his viciousness. For that reason he could not have him there. He stated further that if I would go after him he would employ all the help I would need and pay me well for doing so.

When I arrived at the farm I was surprised to find

such an extraordinary vicious animal. He was tied with a very heavy rope in a box stall; had not been out of that stall for about a year.

Not finding a suitable enclosure to give him the "bluff act," and teach him that I was his superior, I had to resort to the following plan: I took a long strap, made a stationary loop around his neck and a half hitch around the lower jaw. I did this while in the high manger, and that too at great risk. I then took the end of the strap on the outside of the stable, when he came at me on his hind feet, striking; but when he came within four or five feet of me I discharged a blank cartridge from a thirty-eight caliber revolver. The desperate brute was taken by such surprise that he jumped about five feet high, and nearly fell down. I had a helper stir him once more; when I discharged another cartridge in front of him, when he showed some signs of having enough of trying to jump on me. After one or two more shots he had no inclination to run after me. Although he could not be approached yet, he was safe to lead into town, where we turned him loose in the tent ready for his thorough subjection, where he proved to be a test case. I commenced on him at eight o'clock and worked on him until after nine, but did not reach unconditional submission. Knowing it would be best for the horse to rest before another lesson, I suggested finishing the work privately the next day, all members of the class having the privilege of witnessing the performance. The following day we began on him again, when his resistance became so desperately obstinate that he would stand and kick at his tail. No method of subjection was equal to the emergency, except extreme pressure on the spinal cord (which you will find explained elsewhere in this book.) I removed the roll for a short time, then applied it once more, when he showed unconditional surrender. The next day he was curried in his stall without a string or strap on him.

There are numerous other "Noted Cases" that I would like to call your attention to, but space will not permit at this time.

While this book is not a large one, it contains more information on training horses than almost any other book published on the subject. There are other larger books that are said to be horse training books, yet are largely made up with Veterinary departments and other reading matter that does not pertain to the education of the horse at all. I am often asked why I don't study Veterinary Surgery in connection with horse training. My answer is simply this: I have already undertaken all that is possible for one man to master. "Horse training" and "horse doctoring" are two different professions, and are as far apart as farming and practicing law. And in my estimation it is impossible for any one man to thoroughly master two professions. He will invariably make one secondary to the other, and in most cases he will make a complete failure of both. It has been my full desire and aim to thoroughly master the art of controlling and educating horses; consequently I have dropped every thing else.

I have devoted and always intend to devote my whole time to the profession of horse training. Therefore those who read this little book will not need to expect anything but solid, practical information pertaining to the disposition, the vices and education of the horse.

When it is engaged in with the sense of responsibility, care and skill which it demands, it is in reality worthy of being ranked among the most important, interesting and elevating of the professions.

Any special information desired on the management of the horse, can be obtained through my address, Pleasant Hill, Ohio.

Your Obedient Servant,
JESSE BEERY.

ADDITIONAL PRESS NOTICES.

Since the foregoing was in type complimentary press notices have been sent to me in great numbers, a few of which are presented, as coming from different localities.

From Illinois.

HORSE TRAINER CLASS.—100 MEMBERS IN DECATUR—
EXHIBITIONS NIGHTLY IN THE TENT ON SOUTH
WATER STREET.

Prof. Jesse Beery, the famous trainer of the most fractious horses which can be found, is now giving exhibitions every evening in the big tent at the corner of South Water and Jefferson streets. He has a class of 100 members. All were present last night when, through the manager, Mr. Coffeen, Prof. Beery was formally introduced. The Professor with wonderful power handled kickers, balkers and runaway horses, demonstrating that his methods are well worth adoption. His system of colt training was an eye-opener to horsemen present who had thought they knew it all. The lecture by the Professor on how to handle horses should be heard by everybody who owns or controls a horse.

The class is quite enthusiastic over the opportunity afforded it to gain useful knowledge. They want their friends to visit the tent, and by permission of the Professor all who call tonight or any evening during the engagement will be admitted. Don't fail to see Prof. Beery. He is the king of trainers.

From Bloomington, Illinois.
SCHOOL OF HORSEMANSHIP.

H. T. C. Coffeen, the advance agent and press manager of Prof. Jesse Beery, the unrivaled horse trainer, has already secured a class of more than fifty in the city, who will begin a course of instruction under the Professor next Tuesday evening. As an evidence of what is being done by Prof. Beery elsewhere we take our excerpt from a letter of recommendation signed by a large number of the best citizens of Bloomington, Ill. It reads as follows:

'We are highly pleased and perfectly satisfied with

our instruction and with the Professor as a teacher. He has in every instance accomplished completely everything he has attempted, thoroughly subduing and teaching the horse better habits than previously possessed of. The Professor has in every way, while here, conducted himself as a gentleman worthy of our confidence in him in his chosen profession. This testimonial is given unsolicited and unknown to the Professor."

From Springfield, Illinois.

BEERY AND HIS COLTS.—AN INTERESTING SCHOOL FOR HORSES—LAST NIGHT'S PERFORMANCE.

In the vacant lot just east of the city hall there stands a tent. It belongs to Prof. Jesse Beery, who is giving instructions in horse training. Last evening the tent was well filled with both ladies and gentlemen, who took great interest in the work with the young colts.

The first animal was a 2-year-old belonging to John Lauck. The colt had never been harnessed, or even bridled, but it was not long before Beery had it under complete control. George Hofferkamp's 3-year-old was the next one, and as it is part broncho and part something else, and has a penchant for kicking, the audience looked for some sport, and they were not disappointed.

From Fort Wayne, Indiana.

HORSE TRAINING AND TAMING—PROF. BEERY DELIGHTS A LARGE AUDIENCE WITH HIS EXHIBITION LAST EVENING.

Every seat beneath the large canopy was crowded with ladies and gentlemen last evening to witness the exhibition of Prof. Beery's system of colt training and horse taming, and so large was the attendance that many were forced to stand throughout the evening.

The first subject introduced was a highly bred filly, the property of Prof. L. A. Worch. This animal proved to be an apt pupil, and very promptly responded to all the professor's requirements.

The second subject was a most vicious and intractable 4-year-old colt, the property of Mr. M. W. Fitch. A struggle, lasting over an hour, resulted in the subjugation of the headstrong animal, which evinced a determination to give up the battle for supremacy.

From Jackson, Michigan.

HORSE FLESH SUBDUED.—PROF. BEERY CONQUERS THE EQUINE WITHOUT MALTREATMENT.

Prof. Beery worked and lectured before a good audience at the tent on North Jackson street last evening. The first to interest the lover of the horse was the subduing of a vicious 3-year-old colt which nearly killed a man at the farm near Michigan Center. The method taught proved successful, and the colt at last was as gentle as a kitten. An ugly horse which for years has objected to being haltered and harnessed was next shoved through the process of obedience, and the entertainment concluded with an exhibition by the Professor's trained horse.

From Logansport, Indiana.

KICKER FROM KICKERVILLE.—VICIOUS HORSE FINELY HANDLED BY PROF. JESSE BEERY.

Prof Beery, the horse trainer began his school here last night. His first lesson demonstrates that he is an adept—a master of his business. Firmness, followed by kindness, is his manner of handling the colt or vicious horse. He had two subjects last evening which finely illustrated his skill. One was a two-year-old colt, owned by Agent Newell, of the Wabash, which had never been handled before; the other, a splendid looking mare, owned by Dr. Lybrook, of Young America, which was known as a "kicker from Kickerville." The kicker had conquered all the horse talent from Deer Creek and had been turned out to grass by the well known physician as a useless and vicious piece of horseflesh. A half hour under the Professor's management and he had the animal under complete control. The Professor impressed all who witnessed his performance as being a trainer of superior merit and he will doubtless have a big run of business during his stay here. This is his second appearance in Logansport.—Logansport Reporter.

From Springfield, Ohio.

The average person would not think that the breaking of colts and training of horses would prove a popular entertainment. Yet Prof. Jesse Beery, of Pleasant Hill, O., during his two week's stay in this city practically and potently demonstrated that not only professional horsemen, but all intelligent owners and lovers of horses are deeply interested in the subject of, breaking, training, and caring for horses, and respond quickly and liberally to a humane, kindly, and efficient system of horsemanship.

Prof. Beery organized a large class, including men of all vocations, to whom he imparted his system of horsemanship. But his public exhibitions during the past two weeks deeply and widely aroused popular interest, and his tent was nightly crowded with ladies, gentlemen and children, all intently interested in the Professor's work. He first conquers his horse by means of humane and harmless appliances, teaches him that man is the master and that disobedience and viciousness will only hurt him. The Professor's appliances are so constructed that when the horse becomes ugly and disobedient, he punishes himself. Then when he is obedient he is caressed and treated kindly; when he is frightened, he is taught by actual contact that the object or noise will not hurt him.

Prof. Beery subdued and made useful horses out of a number of vicious colts and of older horses with ugly and dangerous habits. He redeemed a number of fine, valuable horses, rendered almost worthless by vicious habits, by breaking them of their habits. The people of this city were especially prepared for Prof. Beery's reformative and enlightening system of horsemanship by reason of a number of serious and several fatal runaways. His work was heartily appreciated and he left a host of friends here who will always gladly welcome him back to Springfield. The seed sown by Prof. Beery's system of horsemanship will bear an invaluable harvest in this city and vicinity.—Springfield News.

From Lancaster, Ohio.

LIKE A CANNON SHOT—WENT THE KELLER HORSE OUT OF PROF. BEERY'S TENT—THE UNTAMED STEED MAKES A BOLT FOR LIBERTY, AND HAULS UP IN FRONT OF EYMAN'S DRUG STORE—A LITTLE FUN NOT ON THE BILLS.

The large audience that assembled last night at the tent of Prof. Beery, the horse educator, was treated to a scene not on the bills, but which redounded to the credit of the horseman. The first horse brought in the ring was one belonging to Mr. Chris. Keller, the groceryman. The horse is noted for running away and smashing things to pieces every time he is hitched up, and is an especially bad case. Prof. Beery gave the class a description of the temperament of the horse as shown by the shape of its head, and said that before he commenced the regular work he would show the class what a vicious brute this horse is. He put on his safety rope and the lines and drove the animal a few times around the ring. He then had an assistant hang a bunch of tin pans to the crupper, for the purpose of stirring the animal's resistance. When he started the horse it didn't do a thing but make a half-circle around the ring and bolt for the door of the tent, which was closed, and he went clear through it. Just as he went through the door the Professor threw him down and as the horse regained his feet he was thrown again, landing on his back. In the fall Prof. Beery was entangled in the guy ropes of his tent, and as the horse came to his feet the trainer was obliged to let go, and a second later the people along Broad street were treated to the sight of a streak of horseflesh going by with two strings of tin pans tied to his tail, and every jump the horse made he kicked the pans up in the neighborhood of the trolley wire. Prof. Beery followed the runaway, which was caught in front of Eyman's drug store, corner Main and Columbus streets. No damage was done outside of breaking a mail box at the corner of Mulberry and Broad streets.

When the audience saw the horse and his trainer shoot out of the tent like a ball out of a cannon the first thought was that the performance was at an end, but those who had been regular attendants and knew something of the indomitable grit of Prof. Beery, knew that if the horse did not kill himself he would be brought back and subdued. Hence the people remained on their seats, and when the Professor came back with the tin pans and in a grave manner announced that the "Keller horse will be subdued tonight" he was cheered to the echo. In a few minutes the horse was brought in and Prof. Beery put him through a course of training that completely subdued him, hitching him up and making him stand still while pistols were shot over him, bells and tin pans pounded around him and flags and paper waved over him.

Prof. Beery explained that this was the first accident of the kind that had befallen him in his nine years of work with vicious horses, and that he was only too glad that no one was hurt.

On account of sickness of serious nature in his family Prof. Beery is obliged to start for home tomorrow morning. Tonight will be his last exhibition here and six horses will be handled before the audience. People who own horses will make a great mistake if they do not purchase one of the books he offers on the subject of colt training and horse management. Come out tonight and see his exhibition.—Lancaster Gazette.

THE LAST PERFORMANCE.—PROF. BEERY, THE HORSE EDUCATOR, CALLED HOME BY SICKNESS IN HIS FAMILY—PLENTY OF BUSINESS FOR TWO WEEKS YET, IF HE COULD HAVE REMAINED— HONEST AND STRAIGHT IN BUSINESS.

Prof. J. Beery, the horse educator, who has been

in Lancaster for the past two weeks, has been called to his home in Pleasant Hill, Ohio, by sickness in his family. He left this morning on the 7:31 train. He has done a very successful business here, and had work enough in view to have kept him busy for the next two weeks. But like every true man, the comfort and care of his family is paramount to all business considerations with Prof. Beery, and so last night he closed his work here. When the audience was dismissed many of our citizens gathered around the Professor and bade him good-bye, congratulating him on his excellent work and assuring him of a welcome should he return to Lancaster.

Prof. Jesse Beery, while not a native of this county, is the next thing to it. His father was born and reared near Bremen, this county, and is well known to the older citizens of that community, although he moved from Bremen to Miami county several years ago. This was Prof. Beery's first visit to his father's native county and it has been one of great credit to himself.

Nearly two weeks ago he came to this city, erected a tent on the corner of Broad and Allen streets, and announced that he would teach people how to educate their horses. His manner of advertising was unostentatious and his statements won him the attention of horsemen. He drove on our streets a beautiful Hambletonian, hitched to a light cart, but without bridle or lines, controlled entirely by the motion of a whip or a sound of the voice.

He had no trouble in getting a large class, and his success in handling all kinds of vicious and spoiled horses is well known to the readers of the local press.

In this day of so many impostors it does one good to be able to notice such honest, capable work as Prof. Beery has given our people, and the highest compliment that could be paid him was the hearty manner in which the members of his class thanked him for what he had taught them, together with the unanimous verdict of the spectators as they agreed with each other that "that man is all right."

One of the features of Prof. Beery's exhibition which received the commendation of all who have been present was the earnest and intelligent work of the young man who assisted the trainer. This young man's name is Roy Coppock and his home is Richmond, Indiana. This is his first season with Prof. Beery, but he has the natural traits of a horseman, and the fearless way in which he took hold of high-spirited horses and laid them down won the admiration of the ladies and the commendations of the men.

Prof. Beery will be welcome when he comes to Lancaster again.—Lancaster Gazette.

Reference having frequently been made to this manual on Colt Training, I gladly give space to one or two of the more recent commendations it has drawn from the press of to-day.
From The Spokesman, Cincinnati, Ohio, June, 1896.

We acknowledge the receipt of a 250-page paper

bound book, entitled "Jesse Beery's Colt Training," illustrating and describing a practical system of colt training and the best methods of subduing wild and vicious horses. Prof. Beery is perhaps to-day the best-known trainer and educator of the horse. His experience is unlimited, having educated and trained some of the most vicious horses before large and appreciative audiences and private classes for instruction; hence he is the man most eminently fitted to prepare a practical training manual. The book is one of the most comprehensive we have ever seen, and we have reviewed many of a similar character in these columns. The theory and practice of training are comprehensively explained and illustrated. Every horse owner should make a study of the plain, common sense manner in which Prof. Beery takes up each individual subject and disposes of it. The book is of especial value to owners of horses possessing a disposition to be disagreeable in any manner whatever. The reading of a single chapter may result in increasing the value of a horse one hundred per cent. The price of the book and other information may be had upon application to Prof. Beery, Pleasant Hill, Ohio.

From The National Humane Educator, Cincinnati, Ohio, June, 1896.

BALKY HORSES.—SOUND DOCTRINE FROM EMINENT AUTHORITY.

The "Coming Man" in "Horse Training" is Prof.

Beery. We were lately in Springfield, O., where he had a two week's entertainment, widely arousing popular interest. His tent was nightly crowded with ladies, gentlemen and children, all intensely interested.

The Springfield Sunday News says: "His work was heartily appreciated, and he left a host of friends who will gladly welcome him back to Springfield. The seed sown by him will bear an invaluable harvest in this city and vincinity."

It is not only his skill and daring which elicits praise, but his humane methods. Even his appliances for subduing the most vicious and dangerous animals, are thoroughly humane in design and effect, yet so ingenious and potent as to give immediate results.

In regard to balking he says: "Horses know nothing about balking until they are forced into it by bad management.

"We must remember that our ways and language are just as foreign and unknown to the horse as any language in the world is to us; we should never get out of patience with them because they do not understand us."

His chapter on Balking in his work on "Colt Training," is worth the price of the book. He describes minutely the causes of balking, and with equal plainness gives the remedy, which every one can understand and use. In conclusion, we are glad of anything that substitutes reason, common sense and humane methods, in place of ignorance and time-honored stupidity. We are glad to hail the dawn of a better day and to herald its coming.

Our columns are open to all such information, not in the interest of any man or set of men, but in helping on the noble cause in which we have embarked so many hopes and ventured so much of time, strength and material resources.

We would also hail with joy, more co-operation and encouragement on the part of many who profess great interest in the cause, but whose conduct is at variance with their profession.

TIMELY FACTS AND MAXIMS

IN ACCORDANCE WITH OUR SYSTEM OF "COLT TRAINING."

THE HORSE.

H. W. Beecher: Society owes to the horse a depth of gratitude a thousand times greater than it does to thousands of men who abuse him. He has ministered to progress; has made social intercourse possible when otherwise it would have been slow and occasional, or altogether impossible; he has virtually extended the strength of man, augmented his speed, doubled his time, decreased his burdens, and becoming his slave, has relieved him from drudgery and made him free. For love's sake, for the sake of social life, for eminent moral reasons, the horse deserves to be bred, trained and cared for with scrupulous care. The teaching of men how to do it has been left too long to men who look upon the horse as an instrument of gambling gains, or of mere physical pleasure.

The famous, rich and powerful Duke of Portland, (Master-of-Horse to the Queen), who is devotedly fond of animals, and one of the leaders in the Animal Cause in England—has lately discarded all check-reins in his great stables and the Queen has followed suit. We hope these illustrious examples will be emulated by the rich and influential of America also, those who love and follow all English fashions, who idiotically use the tight check, "an instrument of torture and device of Satan" as noted English authorities will term it. The Duke and Duchess are foremost in all the great and noble Animal reforms of the day.

J. S. Rarey, the horse trainer, said: "Almost every wrong act of a horse is caused by fear, excitement or mismanagement. One harsh word will increase the pulse of a nervous horse ten beats a minute. Horses know nothing about balking until forced into it by bad management. Any balky horse can be started steady and true in a few minutes. I never found one that I could not teach to start his load in fifteen minutes and usually in three.

Intelligent horsemen have learned that kickers, biters and balkers are natural results of abuse, that not one horse in a hundred is vicious until made so by cruelty; that whipping a horse is as mean and senseless as whipping a baby, and that the most useful, obedient and long lived horses are those treated from birth with kindness and common sense.

"The whip is the parent of stubborness, but gentleness wins obedience. There is no such thing as balkiness in a horse that is kindly treated, and that gets an occasional apple, potato or sugar from his master's hand."—Western Exchange.

Budd Doble, the famous turfman says: "The days of whipping are past and few attempt to force out a horse in that way. Many a driver has lost a race by whipping or spurring which causes sulks. I use only light taps of the whip; when I ride I muffle my spurs."

"Instead of breaking colts we gentle them. The word 'gentle' tells the whole difference between the old method and the new.—H. C. Merwin.

"When a horse is afraid or excited, quiet him by kind words and caress. An excited horse is practically crazy and to whip him is dangerous, foolish and cruel. I have known a single blow of the whip to balk a spirited horse. Whipping a balky horse is barbarous and only increases balkiness."—Benson.

A valuable Chicago horse became so ugly under the whip system that his owner feared to drive him and got rid of him at half cost. The buyer removed check rein, blinders and whip, treated him kindly and he is now a pet of a timid lady who drives him "everywhere."

A disciple of kindness bought a handsome horse in Boston at a quarter his cost because nobody dared to drive him. He got him home with difficulty and began gentle and kindly treatment. He is now a kind, safe, reliable horse which can do 12 miles per hour with the road wagon, and the former owner who lost $300 on him, "can't understand it." Kindness pays!

Make your horse your friend, not your slave.

What can be more touching than the sight of that submissive confidence—the humble obedience with which man is appealed to by those animals that support his life? * * * In man's brutality to these the pathos of the brute's submission is overpowering.—John G. Shortall, President National Humane Association.

APPENDIX.

THE FOREGOING PRINCIPLES APPLIED TO DOGS, ESPECIALLY SHEPHERD DOGS.

From time to time the friend of animals has discussed in a more or less scientific way, the ideas pertaining to them. Perhaps as good authority of a late date as exists is Prof. Shaler, dean of the Lawrence Scientific school at Harvard, and by the way of introduction we cite his statement about the dog, which he says was, the world over, the first living possession of man beyond his own kindred. The dog has been so long separated from the primitive species from which he sprang that we cannot place with any certainty his kinship with the creatures of the wilderness. Like his master, he has become so artificialized that it is hard to conjecture what his original state may have been.

We cannot accept the view that the dog is a domesticated form of the wolf, as some suppose, from the fact that it has been found impossible to domesticate the wolf, and the dog has shown no tendency to revert to the wolf type when allowed to run wild. On the other hand he shows entire hostility to the wolf and all of his kind.

The most reasonable theory is, that the ancestors of the domesticated dog were a species that has entirely disappeared from the wild state.

One thing is true, in all countries the dog is a household pet. He is the chosen companion of all classes of people, and Cuvier gives him the distinction of being the only animal that has followed man over the whole world.

Dogs give faithful and valuable service in return for the protection they receive from their masters. On sheep farms they defend the flocks, guide them from the pastures to the sheepfold, and keep them together if night or storm overtakes them.

The dog is the farmer's best friend; he guards his poultry yard from nightly wanderers, protects his garden and house from thieves, and drives his cattle afield and brings them home.

Innumerable are the stories which tell of life and property saved by the timely warning given by the house dog.

In the cold Northern countries where there are no horses or oxen, dogs are used to draw sleds over ice and snow. In other countries they are used to hunt wolves and other wild animals, and sometimes they are trained to follow criminals.

There is much reason for the assertion that the Shepherd dog, or Collie, is, on the whole, the most highly organized, as he certainly is the most useful of all dogs.

One breed may rise, another fall,
But the Shepherd dog survives them all.

The English Sheep dog or Drover's dog, is of ancient origin, its early history being involved in obscurity. The earliest work on the Shepherd dog was published in 1550.

It was originally written in Latin.

The English dog is heavier and stronger than the Scotch Collie, and the original Spanish Sheep-dog is a very powerful animal. When armed with a spike collar he is a sufficient match for the largest wolves that infest the mountainous parts of Spain. They are very ferocious and will allow no strange person to approach the flock.

A thousand sheep require the attention of two men and two dogs.

The Mexican Sheep dog is descended from the Spanish, but is much smaller, though equally intelligent in his business of watching herds and flocks.

There are now in the United States five different kinds of Shepherd dogs: The Scotch Collie, the German, the Spanish, the Mexican, and the English, sometimes called the bob-tailed, as this is a characteristic of that breed; whether originally tailless, like Manx cats, or because under the old excise laws, all Shepherd dogs without a tail were exempt from tax, (and for this reason removed) is not known.

Of these the Scotch Collie is regarded as the best and is the best known.

Among the moors, fens, glens and hills of Scotland

he is as clannish as his master, and will not make friends with the stranger who stops with the master over night.

"In sagacity he excels all others of the dog family. His is not the superficial intelligence of the mere trick dog; one look into his bright, wise eyes will tell you that antics and pranks are not for him; a dog's life is to him quite too serious a matter to be wasted in frivolities; his mission is hard work; he has duties to perform, as had generations of his ancestors before him.

Indeed, certain parts of Scotland and England owe all their value for sheep raising purposes to the Collie."

We learn from the "Shepherd's Calendar" that "a single shepherd and his dog will accomplish more in gathering a flock of sheep from a Highland farm than twenty shepherds could do without dogs. * * * * * He is the only dog on the farm that earns his bread." In fact the value of a well trained Collie on a large sheep ranch cannot be estimated in dollars and cents.

Since the bench show has come into vogue there has been too much attention paid to mere type. The working instinct is of prime importance, whereas we often see the favorites of the exhibition of no use in the flock.

Breeding alone for show is lowering the standard of usefulness for the Collie, and it is high time the public should be reminded of the recognized standard of a true working Collie, so we will consider a few of his points. The under coat should be thick and the outer coat well developed, though excessive length or weight would only be an impediment to his action.

As brain room is required, the skull ought to be broad and somewhat flat.

The muzzle should be tapering, like that of a fox; and as to his shape, a lithe, free and sweeping form is requisite, that he may go at full speed, no matter how rough the ground, nor what obstacles he may have in his path. He should have a deep narrow chest with moderately long legs. His ears should be small and sensitive, his tail carried low, but long and curling upward toward the end.

His coat is one of the special traits of the breed.

The under coat is of thick, close soft hair and the outer coat of long coarser hair, so that the two together are impervious to rain. There are also smooth coated Collies; the coat depends much upon climate and habits of life. As to colors, some writers claim that the original color was black and white; others say black and tan. It goes without saying that the color is a matter of no real consequence, although at the present time an effort is being made to produce pure white Collies. Most of them have dark ears or spots on the body. A pure white puppy of this breed was once presented to Queen Victoria, who has always been a lover of dogs, and has done more than any other ruler in the world to encourage kindness towards dumb animals.

"The Queen's Collies are very fine, but she loves every species of dog, from the largest St. Bernard to the tiny King Charles Spaniel, which can be put into a coat pocket. There is a man at Windsor Castle who does nothing else but take care of the dogs, and the royal kennels there are of stone, and the yards are paved with red and blue tiles, and the compartments in which the little dogs sleep are warmed with hot water, and they have the freshest and cleanest of straw in which to lie. There are fifty-five dogs in these kennels, and most all of them are acquainted with the Queen. She visits them often while she is at the castle, and she looks carefully after their health and comforts. The dogs of Windsor Castle keep regular hours. They are turned out at a certain time each day for their exercise and sports, and they have a number of courts connected with the kennels, upon which they scamper to and fro over green lawns. There are umbrella-like affairs on these lawns, where they can lie in the shade if they wish to, and in some of them are pools of water where the dogs can take a bath, and in which they swim and come out and shake themselves, just as though they were ordinary yellows dogs, rather than royal puppies."

The disposition of the Collies is as marked as his other traits. Naturally he is all kindness and affection. Yet some writers who think they know all about dogs, tell us that he is of a cross and surly temper. It is true that when out on a desolate moor for days and months he becomes suspicious and distrustful of strangers. But he rules a flock of sheep much as a good horseman controls a horse, by innate "force of character" and not by ferocity. An Australian sheep owner writes of his own ranch and dog as follows: "My own Sancho never did himself as much credit with a small number as with a great many sheep. When I was riding on an endless plain with the flock spreading out two miles, he would watch for me to wave my hand, when all shouting would be lost in the distance. When he was so far off that I could not distinguish him I knew he was looking out for the signal of a fluttering handkerchief to the right or left, and that he could discern a different motion which meant "That will do." When the flock was set in the right direction, he would make a long bend and come to me, and without any orders keep each wing up, first going half a mile to the left, and then as far to the right."

Before winding up this branch of the subject, (after which I propose to illustrate the foregoing theories by an object lesson of my own,) I submit the opinions of another which are so nearly my own that I cannot formulate them better than to quote entire. "The Collie is one of the coming dogs in America. If he were better known and his usefulness on the farm more widely appreciated, he would soon supplant all curs of low degree; and as a faithful, intelligent almost human guardian, he would watch over and attend flocks of sheep in districts where now, because of the midnight forages of mutton hungry mongrels, sheep cannot be raised. They are pre-eminently the farmer's dog, but if anyone is in need of a faithful intelligent servant or companion, let him get a Collie.

His chief charm as a companion is his great affection and strong attachment. * * * * * * * The only faults you will find in him will be his extreme restlessness and activity. He will drive the chickens, stand guard over the geese, here one minute, there the next, looking into this corner and poking his nose into that, forever on the move; but while among all breeds of dogs he can be truly called the policeman, as he is always looking into things, he is not at all too headlong in getting into a scrimmage."—[Wickham.]

TRAINING FOR SPECIAL PURPOSES. HOUSE AND YARD.

A few of the same rules that I have given for colt training apply with equal force to the educating of dogs. Set it down as a fact that no animal will, of itself, perform special duties without special training. They may be more or less gifted by nature, but the technique as artists say, of their business, must be taught them by human agencies.

It requires work to train even a shepherd dog, which is so remarkable for sagacity and willing obedience; but it well pays the owner to bring to his task all the kindness and patience he can command. You cannot afford to hurry or lose your patience in the least.

Remember too, that but one thing can be taught at a time. Secure his affection and respect, and your final success is certain if you know what you want to accomplish, and are complete master of yourself. Some of the treatment to which puppies are subjected by their ignorant, impatient trainers, is simply outrageous and entirely needless.

It is true that a certain amount of coercion is necessary, with young dogs as well as with young people;

but their aptitude for hearing is so great, and they like so well to be taught, that little correction is needed. Never punish him to compel him to learn, or for failure to understand, but only for wilfully refusing to do what he has already learned to do.

Your way of communicating ideas to him is limited, compared with speaking to a child; so do not expect him to learn faster than a child, as so many do expect.

He will understand actions better than words, and whenever possible you should let him see you do whatever you expect of him, freely using your hand in giving directions.

In giving the same order, use the same word every time. For instance, do not say "fetch" at one time, and "bring," at another.

When the lesson, whatever it is, is a failure, the fault is more with the teacher than the pupil.

Take him young, let no one feed or pet him but yourself, until he is thoroughly trained.

The very first thing to teach him is his name, and this should be short and easy to speak.

Teach him to "lie down," to "come," "to speak," and other simple things.

He should have a wide, easy collar, which he ought to wear a while and run about as he pleases. In a few days attach a light chain, still letting him be at liberty, or taking him with you in the fields. But in a few days it will be time to commence guiding and restraining his movements. Take hold of the chain, but at the same time coax him along and reward him with something he likes, whenever he stops pulling at the chain or cord. He will very soon pay no attention to the chain, but keep up with you of his own accord. Never on any account drag him along or break his spirit.

Give him his first lesson among familiar surroundings where nothing will disturb him, that he may give all his attention to the lesson. Teach him first to come to you in response to the order "Come here," only the word "come" will have any significance for him.

Use it when you feed him, and caress him when he responds to the word.

Next teach him to "lie down." This is so easy as to need little explanation. But if he is entirely unable to comprehend it, gently force him down in some natural, easy position, at the same time reiterating the command, "lie down."

Practice will make him drop at the word.

Always reward him with kind words and caresses. If he tries to get up before ordered, go back to him, saying "lie down," going away from him further and further and continuing it till he will lie still till you ... him to "Come," or "Come here."

You may next teach him to "Speak." This you can do by means of a piece of meat (or cheese of which they are unusually fond) which you hold "so near, and yet so far," close enough for him to smell it, but draw it away again, making a whining or barking noise yourself, which in most cases he will imitate. As soon as he makes any attempt to bark, give him the dainty.

If you keep this up day after day it will be but a

few lessons that he will require before he will bark lustily.

As in colt training, do not give one lesson long enough at a time to induce weariness.

One thing cannot be said too often or too impressively: do not be too severe with puppies. The majority of them are only too anxious to be engaged in something to employ their restless activities, and they delight in being made the partner of your pursuits, whatever they are. You will find it necessary to teach him other words, even early in your course of training, such as "Steady," "Stop," "Go on," "Over," and many more, as your lessons progress. The command "over" is wanted to make your dog cross a fence. You first take a piece of board, in height proportioned to the size of your dog, and place a piece of meat on one side, the dog on the other. Have the board so placed that he can get around, but to get the meat he must go over it. He will try to go around, but this you must not allow. After several attempts, the desire for the meat will teach him to jump over the board. This performance you can vary, substituting a stick for the board. Hold the stick higher and higher, but do not ever let him go under. Be sure and praise him when he succeeds in jumping over the stick; he will need no other reward, when he has once learned.

Another important lesson is to teach him to "Come behind," or as the English say, "Come to heel."

The easiest way to do this is to have a stick of the right length with a harness snap in the end of it, which you fasten into his collar ring. With this you can keep him in position, although he will not like it. But be patient with him, talk kindly to him, and as soon as you relieve him tell him to "Go on," which he will be only too willing to do. Eventually you can use a cord in place of a stick, and with a little switch in your hand you can, by a gentle tap, remind him to get back when he tries to push ahead, as he will be sure to do.

This last accomplishment will be found indispensable when you undertake to use you dog in the field; it will save you much wear and tear of voice and temper.

FIELD WORK.

Rule 1.—Go slowly, but persevere.

Rule 2.—Use no harshness; the dog will never forget it.

Rule 3.—Go with him, and show him just what to do.

Rule 4.—If really disobedient, and you must punish him, go to him instead of calling him to you.

Rule 5.—If compelled to correct him, never let him go away till you are friends again; he may run off and be ruined.

Rule 6.—"Like master, like dog." If you are gentle with the sheep, he will be; but if you are rough he will learn to worry them.

Rule 7.—Do not let him follow any teams or persons except those employed by you about the sheep.

Rule 8.—Never take him among the sheep until he is thoroughly trained to "come here" and will obey at the word.

Rule 9.—Train him to notice the wave of your hand whether to right or left, according as you want him to go. This is important, because when it is windy, or he is at a distance, he can see signals when he could not hear you. Sometimes, on a wide plain he can hardly see the hand; it will then be necessary to wave a handkerchief.

Holding it straight up and still, signifies "That will do." Afterwards you can teach him to move slowly to the word "steady."

You can control him if too impetuous, by fastening a long cord to his collar and jerking him up suddenly when he goes too fast, at the same time saying "steady."

Rule 10.—We will say "lastly," although in reality the details in training a Sheep dog to a reasonable degree of perfection would require a volume; but the tenth rule and the first and last of successful training is not to put him to hard work until he has speed and strength to run ahead of the flock or around it. To teach all that can be learned requires great patience, but results will repay you. A young dog is heedless and at times trying, but if he is too severely dealt with you will spoil him. Study his temper, and if you must correct him, be very kind to him afterwards. He will remember both the punishment and the kindness; but if you are generally kind and only severe now and then his affection for you will survive the unpleasantness, and affection must be the real tie between you.

There is a trite saying that "what man has done, man can do." To illustrate the idea of patience and kindness upon which I have harped so much, I will now give some account of my own dog, a female, a pure Scotch Collie, now less than two years old, which I trained from a few months of age, not for general purposes, but for my own special needs. These she has so well subserved that my personal and domestic affairs would be sadly embarassed by the loss of her.

As my house is some distance from the post office, I have taught her to fetch and carry my mail. This is a convenience to me when at home, as it saves much time; being away during the spring, summer and autumn months, it is a necessity that my mail should arrive and depart with dispatch in my absence, and so my wife makes use of Juno as mail carrier.

Animals, like men, are creatures of habit. It is not a very difficult to teach a dog to go on errands. Wherever you wish him to go take him regularly yourself a few times. He will soon learn when you start where it is that you propose to go, and will be apt to run on ahead and get there first.

I took Juno to the post office, introduced her to the postmaster, to whom I explained my idea, giving Juno the letters in a little basket, the handle of which she held in her mouth.

In training a dog for this feat, care should be taken not to have the basket too heavy.

I wrapped the handle of Juno's basket with soft cloth. I am accustomed to send single books (my work on Colt Training) to correspondents, not in the basket, but fastened to it with rubber rings. The basket has a little bell on the under side. When the mail train has been in a few minutes, I take down the basket and the bell tinkles. Juno hears this and comes to the veranda door, all alert for the errand. I open the door, she comes in, pays no attention to visitors, or to the children (of whom she is extremely fond) but attends strictly to business, watching every motion of mine, intent upon her important commission. I place the basket handle in her mouth, open the door and say "Post office" when she bounds away, "swift as an arrow to its mark." Children come out sometimes and want to stop and play with her; but with head erect she redoubles her speed, and much sooner than any biped could go and return, back she comes, to report and get a pat on the head and the "Good Juno," which she expects. So rational a creature is she, that she has learned to connect the whistle of the incoming train with the errand, and if I delay in getting out the basket she becomes restless and walks about the veranda, with the air of one thinking, "I wonder what he is waiting for? Don't he know the train is in?"

Juno performs several tricks. I have not taken the time from my professional business to teach her a great many but such as I have undertaken she knows thoroughly, and will never forget. At an early age she showed a taste for climbing, which I indulged as far as possible. A step-ladder furnished a route to the top of the grape arbor. From this I laid strips of board leading to the stable lower roof. Along this she would go, and as she was not yet satisfied, I nailed cleats to uprights which I set against the gable of the high barn. On top of this high roof is a square tower with a low railing around its upper part or floor. Juno goes to the top of this tower at command, lies down facing me, with her fore-paws hanging over, waiting for me to say "That'll do," which is the signal for her to come down. As she enjoys it so well I sometimes stop her mid way and say "Repeat," which she does at once.

When the weather is very cold or it is icy on the roofs, I am very careful not to require too much of her. Many are surprised to see how quickly, yet how carefully she makes the ascent and descent. My little son can also send her up and call her down. So many people say "How I would like to have a dog like that!" Very few people would be willing to take the pains to ensure the result. There is much in nature; there is still more in education. As the weather is often unfavorable for out door training, I have a room in my house in which to train and exercise Juno in her lessons.

I have arranged a teeter-board on which she and my little son teeter up and down. Anyone wishing to arrange such a board, (and it is great fun for boy and dog and spectators) must never omit several precautions; an important one is to have a little moulding all along both edges of the board at the dog's end, so that he cannot slide off sideways; and a little chair is a good method of securing the boy's seat. Take off the legs of the chair and fasten it firmly to the end of the board, with the back at right angles to it. An arm-chair is best.

In the middle of this room, vacant except for the exercising apparatus, is a low platform, three or four feet square, eight or ten inches from the floor.

This is the goal, or station, to and from which Juno's exertions are made. When she enters the room, she goes at once to that, and waits for orders.

There is a high-backed chair, also, in one corner of the room, into which, at the word, she gets, and putting her fore-paws on the back, she hides her face to say her prayers. Like some other careless and perfunctory worshippers, she now and then peeps out to see what others are doing. But she never gets down, no matter how much I walk about and talk to her, till I say "Amen."

She plays ball, catches my hat, wears a costume, walks on her hind legs, and does many other things with the greatest interest and eagerness. Any and all of these tricks (and they may be varied almost indefinitely) are taught with ease after the first fundamental idea finds a lodgment in her brain, that is, that she must understand and obey, especially obey. Always reward your dog, both with words and some little treat of which it is fond, after a lesson or practice hour. The kind words are the most important. And you can teach him almost anything you care to, without punishment. Encouragement and petting will do wonders.

One frequent cruelty practised, is that of keeping a dog chained. A chain on a dog is like an overcheck on a horse, only evil and that continually. Think of the misery caused to an active dog to be fastened to a chain, frequently a short one, in every kind of weather.

How often do we hear the pleading bark or the whining of some dog, made unhappy by being chained up, alone.

Dogs are fond of human companionship and a vicious dog that cannot be trusted to run about had much better be humanely killed than to drag out a wretched existence at one end of a chain. Generally it is this very tying up that makes him vicious.

A humane leaflet I saw recently most truthfully says: "People say, if he is loose he will run away." To be sure he will, to keep from being chained up again. Or, "he is chained as a guard, to bark at tramps." But then if he barks all day whether there are tramps or not, he ceases to be listened to, and every one knows how to keep out of the way of a chained dog, or quiet him by a piece of poisoned meat thrown near him.

There is always danger, especially in hot weather, that a tied up dog will suffer from neglect.

People who know that he requires food and clean water, are often too careless to give it to him—water, especially, and the constant thirst which comes from barking and fretting is so great that these careless people would nearly go crazy if they had to suffer it themselves.

There are other, and very serious reasons, which a

veterinary surgeon could explain, that make it essential to the health of a dog, that he should have his liberty several hours each day. There is a kind of grass that a dog eats which has great medicinal value for him, and his instinct alone tells him where to find it when he needs it. When tied up he goes without it, and suffers in consequence.

The best way to keep a dog that needs restraint, is to put him in a yard with a high fence. If this is not practicable, fasten a wire across any yard; on this put an iron ring, which, when attached by a cord to his collar, will allow him to run backwards and forwards, the full length of the wire. The yard ought to have shade as well as sunshine to protect him from too great heat of the sun.

Also a dog's house should be made with a partition running nearly across it, behind which he will be protected from the wind.

It should be raised a few inches from the ground to prevent dampness, which is one cause of mange, and of the disease called "Kennel Lameness." Then there should be a sliding panel in the back of the house to let in sun and air when the kennel needs ventilation and drying. Give your dog clean straw, or better still, clean pine shavings for a bed.

The cutting of a dog's tail and ears is a barbarous practice, and is not only very cruel, but liable to cause serious disease—deafness and canker often follow an exposure of the inside of the ear.

A dog's ears should never be pulled either in play or for punishment, for it may cause deafness. A good combing and brushing is more useful than a bath. Never use hot water for washing dogs; it should be a little warm only. Do not allow a dog who is fond of water to go in too often after a stick; his ambition is beyond his strength, and a dog that dislikes water ought never to be thrown into it. If your dog should be cross and irritable, seek for the cause.

Perhaps it is improper food, or a tight collar or something else that you can remedy. Dogs are very sensitive and respond with pleasure to a kind word, while harsh ones makes them miserable. The great Landseer, the famous painter of animals, owed much of his wonderful success, not only to his genius, but to his love for the animals themselves. He was always partial to dogs and seemed to picture their joys and sorrows in a manner far more eloquent than words. A lady once asked the artist how he learned so much about dogs? "By peeping into their hearts," was his reply. Dogs that he had never seen before would rush up to him with every indication of delight.

A dog should be fed regularly twice a day. His food should be varied; meat and bones entering into it. but too much meat is injurious, and all their meat should be cooked. In summer boil a cabbage with it now and then; it is a good antidote against the mange. Unless he has considerable exercise you should not feed too abundantly.

Mrs. Harriet Beecher Stowe was very fond of dogs, and always had from one to three about the place. After she became famous she kept servants, and one occasion asking the girl whose duty it was to feed the dogs, if they were not hungry, she replied: "No ma'am, I guess not; I fed them all they could eat day before yesterday."

If your dog should have a fit, do not let him get out on the street, or some stupid person may raise the cry of "mad dog" and he may be shot.

Put him into a quiet, dark place, wet his head often with cold water, and a few hours after he has recovered feed him on bread and milk. I once knew a dog that had been fed on salt fish and accidentally shut in where he could get no water. He became almost crazy and scared people nearly into fits, till one of those persons who have brains and use them came along, and said "give him water to drink." He drank half a gallon in a few minutes and then licked the hand that gave him the bowl of water.

A great deal of nonsense has been said and written about mad dogs. In thirty years only two deaths from hydrophobia have occurred in the populous city of Boston. A great many more persons are struck by lightning. If your dog chances to eat anything thrown out to poison rats, give him raw eggs, one after another, and put warm milk with a spoon, far back on his tongue, closing his jaws with the other hand, so that he will be compelled to swallow it.

"BIRD DOG."

This somewhat vague title is usually, in this country, applied first to the setter and next to the pointer, both of which are so generally used for hunting purposes.

There are, however, many varieties of dogs which are so used. Of the setter and pointer there are several varieties, most of them too well known to need description. As no one can prove, even if he so contends, that "sport," so-called, is as important as farming, or as the protection of the home, so neither the setter or the pointer is as useful as the collie.

Some breeds of setters are very handsome. They can be trained to domestic pursuits, and make nice pets, when kept clean; they are not, however, as affectionate nor as sagacious as the collie.

THE ST. BERNARD.

is wonderfully adapted to rescue work in localities where such work is needed.

He derives his name from St. Bernard, of Menthon, who founded there a Hospice nine hundred years ago, for the shelter of travellers between Italy and Switzerland. In the midst of a wilderness hundreds of thousands of travellers, during all these centuries, have found within its hospitable walls genial welcome, rest, food, light and fellowship. The St. Bernard dogs are trained to search in the snow for travellers, and they are wonderfully heroic and successful. Being very large and strong they can drag a man quite a distance, and when compelled to stop will bark for assistance. Many a life has been saved through their efforts.

THE NEWFOUNDLAND

dog, though not nearly as large, is larger than the collie, and as much at home in the water as a quadruped can be. He knows no greater pleasure, apparently, than to rescue some one from drowning, and to be petted and caressed for the act. There are several hundred species of dogs all of which have their good traits and their admirers. Volumes might be written about them, and of the extraordinary feats of which they are capable.

Every day, in ordinary life, we see examples of true fidelity and heroism. They are so common as hardly to be thought noteworthy. We should never come to a conclusion if we tried to recount all the heroic deeds of this valuable companion of man. Be kind and just to the dog; if he is good and faithful, reward him; if he has faults, kindly and patiently educate him out of them. There is no friend so faithful, no watchman so keen, no detective so alert as he, and there is much we may learn from the society of dogs. At least we can learn constancy, sincerity, simplicity and the hatefulness of selfishness, and the man who hates dogs must have something wrong about him.

One of the signs of the times and an encouraging one to humane people generally, is the increasing tendency on the part of the secular and religious press to publish anecdotes and other articles concerning dogs, designed to exploit their noble traits. Some of the best minds of the age do not hesitate to pay tribute to their virtues. From Sir Walter Scott and Cooper to the present time there are not wanting noble minds to recognize the fact that the Creator of all things has endowed them with gifts, which under wise training, do honor to the Almighty's handiwork.

One of the most touching and yet dignified acts illustrating the saying "the greatness of a man consists in doing little things with a great mind" occurs to me in this connection.

A friend of mine, William P. Buell, of Richmond, Ind., (the well-known evangelist and missionary lecturer,) has a fine Collie, nine years old, which he raised from a puppy of a few weeks old.

Being of splendid pedigree and exceptionally well trained, she is a great pet, not only of the family, but of all who know her. Being very sick all one night with symptoms of poisoning, Mrs. Buell went in the morning to the office of Dr. Hibberd (the distinguished president of the American Medical Association, which numbers a hundred thousands members) asking him if he could tell her what to do; at the same time apologizing for asking advice about a dog. I think Dr. Hibberd's re 'v was grand, though quite in keeping with the tenor of his life, full of kind acts, (no one during his life can realize their number,) when he replied: "I am only too glad to relieve suffering in any form, and you can go home; I will find out what to do and let you know." In a short time he drove to the home of the Buell's, and gave full and complete directions for treatment; which being carefully followed, the beautiful and valuable animal was soon as well as ever. It is in the interest of humane and kindly consideration for animals, and also to record such a lofty example of compassion, unalloyed by the petty idea of unprofessional condescension which would have prevented a man of small caliber from driving out of his way for a four footed sufferer, that I have used a personal illustration. The parties are so well known that publicity will not harm them, and that it may be a stimulus to the timid and faint hearted friend of animals, as well as a tribute of "honor to whom honor is due," is my wish and object in relating the incident.

Moral courage is needed in the world in all departments of life; in none more so than in humane work and the training of animals by humane methods, in distinction from the old time "breaking" customs. Read the anecdotes which follow, only a few of the multitudes that might be given, and see what others are thinking and doing in this "end of the century," along such lines.

THE POWER OF ANIMALS IN EXPRESSING EMOTIONS—WHY DOGS WAG THEIR TAILS.

Few animals excel the dog in the power of expressing emotion. This power is a sure sign of an animal which is habitually in communication with its fellows for certain common ends. There are many reasons for the tail being the chief organ of expression among dogs. They have but little facial expression beyond the lifting of the lip to show the teeth and the dilation of the pupil when angry. The jaws and contiguous parts are too much specialized for the serious purpose of seizing prey to be fitted for such purposes as they are in man. There is no doubt that hounds habitually watch the tails of those in front of them when drawing a covert. If a faint drag is detected the tail of the finder is at once set in motion, and the warmer the scent the quicker does it wag. Others, seeing the signal, instantly join, and there is an assemblage of waving tails before the least whimper is heard. When the pack is at full cry upon a scent the tails cease to wave, but are carried aloft in full view.

THE QUESTION OF TAIL-WAGGING.

The whole question of tail-wagging is a very interesting one. All dogs wag their tails when pleased, and the movement is generally understood by their human associates as an intimation that they are very happy. The chief delight of wild dogs, as with modern hounds and sporting dogs, is in the chase and its accompanying excitement as consequences. When the presence of game is first detected is invariably the time when tails are wagged for the common good. The wagging is an almost invariable accompaniment of this form of pleasure, which is one of the chiefest among the agreeable emotions when in a wild state, owing to some inosculation of the nervous mechanism, which at present we cannot unravel; the association of pleasure and wagging has become so inseparable that the movement of the tail follows the emotion, whatever may call it forth.

An explanation of a similar kind may be found, from the fact that dogs depress their tails when threatened or scolded. When running away the tail would be the part nearest the pursuer, and therefore most likely to be seized. It was, therefore, securely tucked away between the hind legs. The act of running away is naturally closely associated with the emotion of fear, and therefore this gesture of putting the tail between the legs becomes an invariable concomitant of retreat or submission in the presence of superior force.— Indianapolis News.

DOGS VERY SENSIBLE TO RIDICULE.

Another extremely human characteristic of the dog is his susceptibility to ridicule. Only in the more sensitive natures of men do we find contempt, expressed in laughter of the kind that conveys that emotion, as keenly and painfully appreciated as among dogs. It is possible, Prof. Shaler asserts, to drive certain hounds away or to quell their anger by laughing in their faces. But once you have cowed a dog by insistent laughter, you can never hope to make friends with him.

"A year or two ago," says Professor Shaler, "I was imprudent enough to laugh at a very intelligent dog in my neighborhood, he having unreasonably assaulted me at my house door, where he had been left a long time to wait while his owner was within, and had thereby been brought into an unhappy frame of mind. Sympathizing with his situation, I preferred to laugh him out of his humor rather than to beat him with my stick. I regret that I did not take the other alternative, for I made the poor brute my implacable enemy by my pretense of contempt for him.

Only a short time since, I knew of a case in which a whole family would have been burned to death in their house, in the night, if the dog had not barked and waked them; and of another case, in which a whole family would have died in the night from coal gas which was coming out of the stove, if the dog had not barked and waked them.

There are many books filled with stories about the good things dogs have done, and many other books might be filled with other stories just as good. They have always been the friends and companions of human beings, and are generally very kind to children. The great naturalist, Cuvier, who studied this whole subject, thinks that men could spare any other animal better than they could spare dogs.

Some of the greatest and best men that have ever lived have been very fond of them. Such men as Sir Walter Scott and Sir Edwin Landseer. And poor men often find them their best friends. A poor, sick colored man, sometime since, travelled on foot hundreds of miles to the hospital at Louisville, Kentucky, to see if he could get cured, having with him his dog. But when they told him he must abandon his dog and turn him into the street, because they would not have any do in the hospital, the poor man took the dog in his arms, and with tears running down his face, said he would rather die with his dog than turn him into the street and go to the hospital. I am glad to say that when they found how much he loved the dog, they let the dog go into the hospital with him.

A traveller in Portugal purchased a native dog, which soon became much attached to him. When spoken to in English, even accompanied by the most expressive looks and gestures the master could command, the dog appeared puzzled, and he seldom found out what was required of him, but when his master addressed him in Portuguese—badly as his master spoke it, the dog joyfully executed his wishes.

After a time by repeating the words alternately in Portuguese and in English, the dog learned the latter as well as the former, and would obey as readily. But the same command given in French reduced him to a state of despair again.

Afterward the dog was carried to France. After living there some time he became so familiar with the language that he understood directions given to him, though—perhaps because he had grown older and a new language was harder to acquire—he never responded so readily as to commands in Portuguese and English.

I once saw a little boy take a splendid medal in Paris, France, in this way: On his way to school with his little dinner basket he came across a poor, half-starved dog, and he pitied the dog so that he just opened his dinner basket and gave the dog all his dinner, and went without himself.

The French society for the prevention of cruelty to animals heard of it and awarded him a medal, and I was present at the annual meeting of the society, in the great hall of the Sorbonne, when the medal was presented.

When the little fellow's name was called and he came forward to get the medal, the whole vast audience of French men and women stood up and cheered him.
—Geo. T. Angell.

CAN DOGS TALK?

When engaged in locating a railway in New Brunswick, James Camden, a civil engineer, was compelled one night by a severe snow storm to take refuge in a small farm house. The farmer owned two dogs, one an old Newfoundland and the other a Collie. In due time the farmer and his family went to bed, the Newfoundland stretched himself out by the chimney corner, and Mr. Camden and the man with him had rolled themselves in their blankets on the floor in front of the fire.

The door of the house was closed by a wooden latch and fastened by a bar placed across it. Mr. Camden and his man were just falling asleep when they heard the latch of the door raised. They did not get up immediately, and in a short time the latch was tried again. They waited a few minutes, and then Mr. Camden rose, unfastened the door and looked out. Seeing nothing, he returned to his blankets, but did not replace the bar across the door.

Two or three minutes later the latch was tried the third time. This time the door opened and the Collie walked in. He pushed the door back, walked straight to the old Newfoundland and appeared to make some kind of a whispered communication to him. Mr. Camden lay still and watched. The old dog rose and followed the other one out of the house. Both presently returned, driving before them a valuable ram belonging to the farmer, which had become separated from the rest of the flock and was in danger of perishing in the storm. Now, how did the Collie impart to the other dog a knowledge of the situation unless through some supersense unknown to us?—Ex.

A Lewiston (Me.) man has a dog which can not only take care of himself, but the property of his owner and other people as well. He pays no fare on the railroads. If he happens to be up in New Hampshire with his master and wants to go home he boards a train and curls up under a seat, and stays there until it is time to change cars; and in a few hours he is found entering the Lewiston restaurant as if it was nothing strange that he had travelled without a protector or guide. In a day or two he will disappear and show up in Lancaster, N. H. He is the same dog that stopped a runaway in Lewiston one time by seizing the rein near the bridle in his teeth and dragging down the horse's head.—Humane Educator.

A NOBLE DOG AND A GRATEFUL CAT.

Mr. Gilmore, of Cedar Rapids, said to a friend one day, "I want to tell you about our dog and cat." The cat had been an inmate of his house for years, and had come to feel as if she were the head of the family. One day Mr. Gilmore brought a big dog home. For a long time the dog tried earnestly to make a friend of the cat, but she would only spit at him and scratch him with her claws. Finally he seemed to give up trying any longed. One day the cat was lying comfortably on the lawn in the sunlight, when suddenly a large, yellow dog jumped over the gate and had nearly reached her, when the old house dog bounded off the porch and his teeth closed in the strange dog's neck. One strong shake sent the intruder away howling with pain. The old dog marched back to his place on the porch and laid down again. The cat got up from her place on the grass and looked at him; walked toward the steps and look again. The old dog lay with closed eyes, and gave her no attention. She stood on the first step and looked at him again. Then she worked her way up to the porch floor, but the dog never moved. Finally she went and laid down between his great fore paws and put her face close to his. "And," said Mr. Gilmore, "that dog and cat have been like David and Jonathan ever since." All the cat needed was knowledge of the dog's nature, which hitherto she had lacked. She had already misjudged him, but just as soon as she realized that he was a noble, true and brave old friend, she gave herself to him with all her heart.

THE BEERY TRAINING APPLIANCES.

Few horse owners realize what it means to have a set of my appliances. If you have, or ever expect to have, a colt to break, the use of these appliances will enable you to do the work in half the time, with less harshness to the colt than any other plan, and make a more valuable horse out of him. If any horse you now own, or may own in the future, has any annoying habit, the use of these appliances, will completely cure him in an incredibly short time. You will realize that it is one of the best investments you ever made. They are made of good leather and sewed throughout—not a rivet in them.

The appliances are divided into three groups, and if you do not care for all the parts, the first and second groups are sufficient to subdue any horse. The first group is simply invaluable in training a colt or taking the conceit out of a horse that has a bad habit of any kind. There are many "family horses" with some little annoying habit that they endure because they think it can not be cured. With these appliances the habit can be removed. Considerable **profit** to the owner of a set of these appliances can be made by a moderate charge for the use of them in the neighborhood.

ALL KINDS OF HORSES,

the wild, vicious—the regular "man-eater" kind, the tricky and dangerous biters and kickers, the shyers at street cars and automobiles, horses that won't stand quiet, horses that do not obey instantly the command "Whoa," horses afraid of umbrellas, horses that do not drive single as well as double, those that pull on the bit, etc, etc.

There is no habit, I care not of how long standing, that can not be removed by these appliances—and that **permanently**. Any horse, no matter how powerful he may be, is rendered completely helpless, and is brought absolutely under control. They should be in the stable of every horse owner.

Booklet giving full description and prices sent on request.

JESSE BEERY, Pleasant Hill, Ohio.

BIT DEPARTMENT.

www.ingramcontent.com/pod-product-compliance
Lightning Source LLC
Chambersburg PA
CBHW031955230426
43672CB00010B/2155